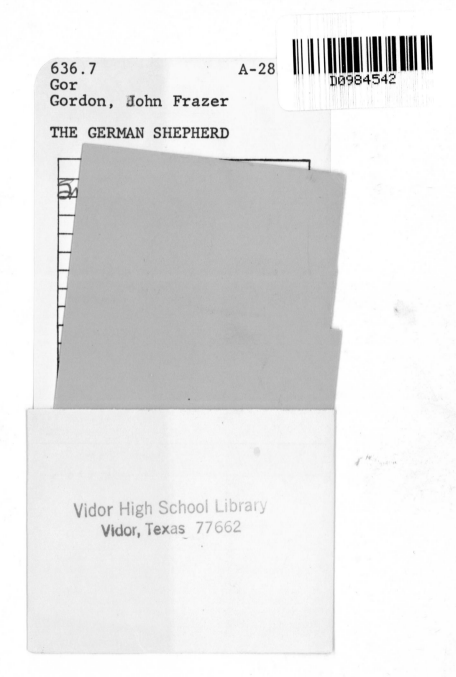

Novem Bacarolle
Owned by Messrs
Woods and Gilmot
(Photo: Diane Pearce)

The German Shepherd Dog
(The Alsatian)

ARCO PUBLISHING COMPANY,INC

New York

Published by Arco Publishing Company, Inc.
219 Park Avenue South, New York, N.Y.

Printed in Great Britain

Library of Congress Cataloging in Publication Data
Gordon, John Frazer.
    The German Shepherd.

Bibliography: p.
    Includes index.
    1. German shepherd dogs. 1. Title.
SF429.G37G65   636.7'3   77–1818
ISBN O–668–04285–0

Contents

CHAPTER 1

Origin and History

The race of Shepherd Dogs is said to stem from the early Bronze Age, thereby making it some 6000 years old. Over this long period it has spread widely, and now its various types extend to virtually every country in the world. Even the Arctic regions have their Shepherd Dogs; these come from the ancient Spitz branch of the family and watch flocks and serve man in many different ways.

The dog we know as the German Shepherd Dog or Alsatian is one of the great family of dogs. Though his present type is not an ancient one, it has developed over countless generations, fashioned by breeders whose aim was to achieve perfection at first as a working dog, and in later years as a show dog. Early writers selected as proof of the breed's antiquity its rather vague resemblance to the limestone sculpture of a dog found in the ruins of Lycopolis, ancient city of the Nile in the days of Amenophis IV, c.1322 **B.C.** Dogs of similar type are depicted in the relief art on the pottery of some Mediterranean lands from about 600 **B.C.,** but frankly the only resemblance between the Egyptian dog and the German Shepherd Dog is in its erect ear carriage: in other features the similarity is only very slight. In view of the fact that good ear carriage in German Shepherds is a comparatively recent achievement, the point can hardly be claimed in support of a clinical relationship. More likely, the limestone dog depicts Anubis, the Egyptian Dog of Reincarnation, a dog which flourished in the days of the Pharaohs; in fact, we call them Pharaoh hounds today, and those who know them (or their cousins, the Ibizan Hounds) will doubt the possibility of any affinity between the breeds. On the other hand, more indicative of the breed's great age is the fact that skeletons of Shepherd Dogs and early sheep types have been unearthed in Europe, suggesting that these dogs existed at least four centuries before the birth of Christ.

Early Development in Germany

Some early authors seem to accept the theory that the German Shepherd Dog originated from a wolf or from crossings involving that animal. But no one now treats the possibility of lupine blood infiltration with any seriousness. Matings between dog and wolf are of course quite possible, and occasionally proof

9

and photographs have been produced in order to substantiate these claims of procreation. However, most recorded modern unions have proved sterile, and there is absolutely no proof available to show that wolf blood exists or existed in the German Shepherd Dog however far back one cares to research. In his *The Alsatian Wolfdog* (1924) G.Horowitz says that a noted foundation bitch 'Mores Pleiningen' SZ. 159 who was whelped in 1894, had wolf ancestry. However this was subsequently dismissed by contemporary experts. It would therefore seem that, even if the wolf were used to contribute his blood in the very early development of the breed in Germany, when dogs with ferocious guarding instincts were needed, such utilization must have been quite superficial. Certainly today's German Shepherd Dog carries few if any wolvine features in his make—up, neither in his structure nor in his expression, and certainly not in his temperament; for the wolf is sly and treacherous to a marked degree.

In Germany, where the German Shepherd Dog was worked and bred for countless generations before it became known to the rest of the world, the breed was of a type which approximated only very roughly to the show and working breed we now know and admire. Today, of course, the German Shepherd, in common with other modern pedigree dogs, has been 'beautified', although it can be claimed that it has not been spoiled. In the early days of the breed in Germany there were many rag—tag—and—bobtail Shepherd Dogs which lacked any semblance of the grace and elegance we expect to see in the present—day German Shepherd. Specimens were often too stocky or too tall or had coats of mixed length and texture; they were without quality and frequently very diverse in size. Undoubtedly, as the demand for good-looking stock grew, the various types of Shepherd Dogs which conformed to the ideal were carefully interbred. Most of the dogs involved in making the dog we know today came from two main regions. In the pastoral lands of highland Thuringia, now a part of East Germany, the native Shepherd Dog was wolf—grey in colour and was generally endowed with erect ears, two attributes considered indispensable to the breed in the initial stages of its show development. This type, however, was lacking the fine brush tail and sturdiness of the guard-cum-shepherd dog of the Wurttemberg, an area in the southern highlands of West Germany bordering France and Switzerland. This too was an agricultural region where sheep abounded. Here the dog excelled in both swiftness and gait, two qualities which emanated from his naturally good hindquarters. Inevitably, these two good types were fused; the best features of each being utilized and, the bad and the unwanted bred out, resulting in a handsome ideal type of dog. According to the records, von Stephanitz introduced a big Swabian dog named 'Audifax von Grafrath' in 1902 for extra substance.

Some Breed Pioneers

Much of the pioneer work to achieve perfection in the breed was done by two fanciers, Herr Wachsmuth of Hanau and Herr Sparwasser of Frankfurt, who, incidentally, obtained his original breeding stock from Wachsmuth in about 1877. This included two well-known dogs 'Grief' and 'Lotte'. Between them these early breeders fixed the best characteristics of the German Shepherd Dog, thereby producing a type which was to rise to dizzy heights in world popularity in only a few decades.

Several great dogs contributed to the breed's development. Probably the best known, most vital and potent was 'Hektor Linksrhein', bred in 1895 by Sparwasser and bought later by Herr Eiselen of the famour 'von der Krone' kennels at Heidenheim. This dog eventually came into the possession of Kapitan von Stephanitz, author of *The German Shepherd Dog (1923)*. The name of 'Hektor Linksrhein' was later changed to 'Horand von Grafrath' and the cipher 'Z1' which follows his name indicates that his was the first name entered in the breed's *Zuchtbuch* (Stud Book). This dog became a pillar of the breed, as did his litter brother 'Luchs' (Sparwasser) Z155, and both figured in many noted and important pedigrees. 'Horand' was definitely a dog of immense potency, and countless trials' winners have descended from him. His blood passes through another great stud dog, 'Beowulf' Z10, and his brother 'Pilot' Z3, who were by 'Hektor v.Schwaben' out of 'Thekla 1 v.d.Krone', the latter being in fact her mate's half-sister. The strength of 'Beowulf' and also his fame lie in the bitches he produced, these are always a valuable contribution by a stud dog to any breed. Another fine dog was 'Horst v.Boll', who although too big to make his mark in the show world, was extremely typey and very well endowed with bone and true breed temperament. Because he was able to transmit these blessings he proved extremely successful as a stud dog.

Thus it is apparent that some very close in-breeding was conducted in the early days to procure the type desired. However, with their usual sound sense in such matters, the Germans segregated closely-related stock to widely-spaced geographical areas. They introduced genuine working stock bloodlines into the breed and saved it from the dangers of consanguinity.

The Phylax Club

In 1891 Kapitän Reilchelmann Dunau and Count Graf von Hahn set out to form a club which would work for the good of the breed, and the Phylax Club came into being. It lasted only three years, mainly because of the acrimony which persisted between rival factions and regions. In spite of this set−back, the founders were unperturbed and considered that they had introduced many influential and worthwhile people to the German Shepherd Dog world. In 1896 a surge of interest in the breed spread throughout Germany when Doktor Gerland of Hildesheim presented the first *trained* police dogs. Riot−quelling dogs had been used in Germany thirteen years earlier, notably in Hildesheim by Kapitän Schoenherr, who became head of the Prussian Government Breeding and Instruction School of Service Dogs at Grunheide. By 1910, nearly 500 police stations in Germany were using trained police dogs, and most of them were German Shepherd Dogs. By this time the 'S.V.' new club had been flourishing for over a decade. This was *Der Verein für deutsche Schäferhunde,* founded in 1899 and destined to become the largest specialist breed club in the world. It is usually referred to as the 'S.V.': Its original headquarters were in Stuttgart; then it moved to Munich and currently its offices are in Augsburg. The club's membership became vast, and its work for the breed throughout Germany and later throughout the world was exemplary. Shows and trials, even shepherding events, were organized and kept to a high standard. Early 'S.V.' Stud Books were published; and these have proved invaluable especially to present−day students of the breed. A breed Standard was produced which, apart from minor amendments, remains in use today. The club's first president was Herr A.Meyer, the noted Kapitän von Stephanitz succeeding him quite early on. It was under von Stephanitz's influence that the breed began to make an impact upon the canine world. He ran the club with military precision, and without his dedicated domination the German Shepherd Dog and the Club would not be in the strong position they hold today.

In due course *Körungs* (breed surveys) were instigated. These are meetings for German Shepherd Dog fanciers chaired by an expert in the breed called a *Kormeister* who surveys and grades the dogs and bitches brought before him by members. The survey is voluntary and the *Kormeister*, who is in effect a breed warden or examiner, balances each specimen's good points with his bad ones, according to the Standard and the general requirements of the breed. Soundness and temperament play major parts in a dog's make−up, and the animal is judged on these qualities as the examination proceeds and is either passed or rejected at the end. If he is passed, he is awarded a *Kor* certificate. The *Korung* is conducted in a manner which recommends rather than enforces, but it does serve to stabilize breed type and eliminate undesirable characteristics. These meetings are also educative for those attending, and there is little doubt that the high standard of the breed in Germany owes a lot to the honesty and scrupulous care with which they are operated.

The idea of introducing a similar system in Britain has been broached, and Boxer enthusiasts have thought about a similar scheme too. However, it has not met with much success, although one or two German Shepherd enthusiasts have given it a try on several occasions. To the insular British the idea seems to savour of dictatorship, many breeders vow that they would not support it if it were introduced, preferring their own judgement in such matters — a pity, for what has done wonders for German Shepherd Dogs in Europe would no doubt help in Britain too. Virtually every German Shepherd Dog owner in Germany approves of the scheme. If the excellence of the dog in Germany results from such *Korungs,* then surely such functions are good for the breed, whatever the critics may have to say about the system being autocratic or dictatorial. To produce good−quality articles of merchandise or good specimens of livestock, one must have rules, rigid discipline, and intense application to the job in hand. The Germans, natural exponents of such characteristics, have proved how quickly beautiful specimens can be produced.

At the start of the First World War in 1914, the S.V. had a membership of about 6000. By 1923 it exceeded 50,000! There were over 180,000 entries in the *Zuchtbuch,* and a boom was under way — German Shepherd Dogs were wanted all over the world: the breed had 'arrived', and almost every dog-lover wanted to own one of these 'fabulous' sagacious dogs. The German breeders began an intensive breeding programme to fulfil the world-wide demand, which was especially great in Britain and the United States of America.

Early Days in Great Britain

Although one can hardly deny that the elegance and personality of the German Shepherd Dog attracted the interest of the British dog−loving public, it is clear that two additional factors promoted his popularity to almost unbelievable heights. One was the impression this clever and intelligent breed made on British soldiers during the First World War. Used not only by the Germans but also by the French on active service, the German Shepherd proved himself under fire as both messenger dog and Red Cross pack dog. Many of these dogs were brought back to Britain by returning soldiers, and the stories that they told of their great work and sagacity soon got around. Their German antecedents had to be hushed up, for there remained an intense antipathy in Britain to anything which savoured of the erstwhile enemy. Consequently, the name German Shepherd Dog was never used. The fact that to the uninitiated the dog resembled a wolf caused him to be called wolfdog by many, although this was an unfortunate name for a dog whose personality and charm is far removed from anything vulpine. Eventually, the name was changed to Alsatian Wolfdog because some of the dogs came from Alsace—Lorraine, and when Lieutenant—Colonel J.T.C. Moore-Brabazon, M.C.M.P., (later Lord Brabazon of Tara) persuaded the Kennel Club to 'recognize' the breed in 1919, it was registered under that name. Alsatians which had been previously registered as Foreign Sheepdogs were transferred forthwith.

The second boost for the breed came from the United States in the 1920s with the appearance of two canine movie stars, both of whom endeared themselves to the British public. The first was 'Strongheart', a bitch whose real name was 'Etzel von Oeringen', introduced by Bruno Hoffman, owned by Jane Murfin and trained by Larry Trimble. The bitch's appearance and activities on the screen made every American want one like her. One breeder with an eye to business was Lawrence Armour of Green Bay Kennels, Chicago, who imported the sire of 'Etzel' ('Strongheart'), a dog named 'Nores v.d. Kriminalpolitzei', thereby creating an immense demand for that stud's services. Probably better known to the British film—going public of the post—war generation was 'Rin—Tin—Tin', a dog stated to be of uncertain pedigree who emanated from France.

Unfortunately, a great deal of promiscuous breeding took place. This always happens in dogdom when demand exceeds supply. Many breeds which have reached great heights of popularity have been ruined by such irresponsibility on the part of some breeders. Puppies were produced in thousands, and type and temperament went by the board. Many impure litters were produced for the sake of easy money, and too often incidents suggesting breed unreliability were reported and amplified by the national press to the Alsatian's disadvantage.

However, strong and reputable kennels were springing up all over the country. Although pioneers in the breed such as Lady Bateman, whose imported brace 'Gim.v.d.Tiefenau' and 'Lotti' had produced pre—war exhibits, and Mrs R.McMillan, whose three imports from France had helped popularize the breed, were no longer in evidence, stalwarts such as Mr H. Robbins ('Mattesdon') and Mr Percy Whitaker ('Southwold') had laid good foundations in their established kennels for the breeders of the 1920s. Mr Robbins came by his first dog for a pound note at an early Cruft's auction! Later, he bought 'Wolf of Badenoch' from the Duchess of Teck. In Ireland Lady Helen Conyngham and Lady Lambart jointly owned a small but successful kennel; Mrs Leslie Thornton was another who helped to put the breed in the public eye before the boom started.

The bad period for the breed began in the mid−1920s and lasted for rather less than a decade. In 1930 the Kennel Club agreed to innumerable requests that the breed's name should be changed. The word Wolfdog was dropped, and the title became just Alsatian (*GSD*). It is a pity that at this time it was not agreed to conform with the rest of the world and give the dog its true title. German Shepherd Dog, forgetting the name Alsatian once and for all. However, this was not to be, and the old name thus remains, although the change to the true name may now not be too far off.

The great work done by the breed during the Second World War more or less wiped out the ill−deserved reputation earned by the Alsatian in the murky years of the late 1920s. Since the last war, the German Shepherd Dog has surged ahead into new fields of activity. The Kennel Club approved the policy and schedule of exercises graded to working dogs, and the highly absorbing hobby of dog−training soon spread throughout Britain. Because the breed lends itself naturally to training and is well endowed with character and brains, it is much in demand for guard work, police work and as guide dogs. Admittedly, the dogs chosen for these occupations were not all German Shepherds, but they formed the majority of the dogs used. Obedience Training Clubs sprang up all over the country and gave the man in the street a chance to get the best out of his dog and to enjoy the ownership of a well−trained animal. Conversely, the dog himself enjoyed being trained so that he could give satisfaction and pleasure to his master or mistress.

British Clubs

All the specialist breed clubs had become fully established by the thirties and were thriving and heavy in their membership. The first club was inaugurated in August 1918 and merged with the Alsatian League of Great Britain founded in

1924, in 1925. The club was re-named the Alsatian League and Club of Great Britain. The *A.S.P.A.D.S.* (Alsatian, Sheep, Police and Army Dog Society), formed in 1923, is a powerful influence today and devotes itself mainly to the working side of the breed; the word 'Associated' has now replaced the word Alsatian, as the club caters for the owners of other breeds also. An important club is the *BAA* (British Alsatian Association), which is the largest one—breed club in the country, having over sixty branches throughout the British Isles. All are well supported and serve the breed well, as do other specialist clubs in the United Kingdom and Ireland.

The years after 1945 saw the emergence of an active figure in a German named Joseph Schwabacher. He had been incarcerated in the notorious Buchenwald concentration camp from which he eventually escaped and came to England, where he became domiciled. He had been very active in Germany with German Shepherds and at once sought to establish himself with the breed in England. Initially his efforts were frustrated by a number of set—backs, mainly financial. The immediate post—war years in Britain were extremely frugal as far as good breeding stock was concerned, and the animals he managed to acquire were culled by viral infections which were rife in dogdom at that time. Distemper and its several side—effect diseases were 'killers' then, and breeders lost entire kennels because the vaccinations available did not provide total protection. Schwabacher tried to farm out some of his bitches on breeding terms, and eventually he managed to form a respectable kennel under his prefix 'Secretainerie', which became noted in the breed. He wrote *The Popular Alsatian* (1922 and later editions) and numerous useful articles in breed journals as well, and helped many breed people with advice and guidance.

Chapter 2

The Breed Standard

Though the German Shepherd Dog has only one breed Standard, there are different versions, published by the British, one by the Americans and one by the 'parents' of the breed, the Germans. (All three are reproduced in this book). There is no great dissimilarity between them. This of course is a good thing, as it indicates that German Shepherd Dogs are being looked at, bred to, and judged on more or less the same level in the most important geographical regions of dogdom; this bodes well for world–wide breed uniformity.

A breed Standard is a standard of excellence approved and announced as workable by the governing body of every country involved. In the initial breed standard there was a scale of points based on the Kennel Club Standard, which, although it varied according to where it was compiled, purported to help judges. This was doubtful, and unfortunately the system did little more than confuse them! Judging by an arbitrary system of points is not really feasible, as any proficient judge will know, and the method is not approved officially, or by the breed itself. In fact, its only merit is that it gives the judge or fancier an extremely rough guide. The scale of points most frequently used is given here for its 'antique' rather than for any current value.

Nature and Expression	20
General Appearance	15
Gait	15
Bone	7
Back	5
Coat	7
Hindquarters	7
Forequarters	7
Chest	7
Feet	5
Head	5
Total	100

Understanding The Standard

To understand the breed Standard you must read and study it with a first—class living specimen of the breed alongside to which you can refer. A good judge of the breed should have owned a good, even outstanding, specimen at some time or other in his career in the fancy. Otherwise, it is extremely doubtful whether he can truly appreciate the physical virtues and general worth of a German Shepherd Dog. When you have an excellent specimen running around your home, his type, form, substance, characteristics, and gait become impressed upon your conscious and subconscious mind. Then, when you judge, these impressions will be superimposed upon the exhibits standing before you in the ring. Admittedly, you must be flexible enough to realize that you cannot compare too rigidly dogs from other strains and other kennels with dogs (however good) that you have owned. You must perforce allow some leeway in the matter of finer points, otherwise your judgement will quickly become biased. However, it must be remembered that there is only *one* type of German Shepherd Dog and that is the *correct* type. Naturally, you must temper this rule according to the country in which you are judging since there are mild variations to consider in the rules of international judging !

The Standard is intended to be a *guide* only. It is not detailed enough to be much more than this and yet it requires no more detail ! A dog (of any breed) must be judged as a whole. Too much detail causes confusion and too often allows unimportant points to be weighed strongly and wrongly against features which are genuinely important. The S.V.Standard was written and evolved by experts who knew what a *real* German Shepherd Dog should look like; it emphasizes those features which they insisted should be perpetuated. The breed Standard is a target at which the conscientious breeder aims. Having been tested over many generations, it is a good and reliable reference in the search for the perfect specimen. The fact that today German Shepherd Dogs are good—looking dogs of correct and true type speaks for the worth and reliability of the breed Standard. The present—day Standard varies little from the original German draft of 1899 and its transcontinental offshoots. The success it has achieved indicates the importance of allowing it to remain unchanged. Alter it, and the breed will be set back and confused, perhaps only temporarily, but nevertheless such a situation will dishearten and cause lack of interest among dedicated breeders.

The British Breed Standard

Characteristics : The characteristic expression of the Alsatian gives the impression of perpetual vigilance, fidelity, liveliness and watchfulness, alert to every sight and sound, with nothing escaping attention; fearless, but with decided suspiciousness of strangers—as opposed to the immediate friendliness of some breeds. The Alsatian possesses highly developed senses, mentally and temperamentally. He should be strongly individualistic and possess a high standard of intelligence. Three of the most outstanding traits are incorruptibility, discernment and ability to reason.

Dunmonaidh Martinet
owned by Miss D.Scrivenor

(Photo: Diane Pearce)

General Appearance : The general appearance of the Alsatian is a well-proportioned dog showing great suppleness of limb, neither massive nor heavy, but at the same time free from any suggestion of weediness. It must not approach the greyhound type. The body is rather long, strongly boned, with plenty of muscle, obviously capable of great endurance and speed and of quick and sudden movement. The gait should be supple, smooth and long-reaching, carrying the body along with the minimum of up and down movement, entirely free from stiltiness.

Head and Skull : The head is proportionate to the size of the body—long, lean and low cut, broad at the back of the skull, but without coarseness, tapering to the nose with only a slight stop between the eyes. The skull is slightly domed and the top of the nose should be parallel to the forehead. The cheeks must not be full or in any way prominent and the whole head, when viewed from the top should be in the form of a V, well filled in under the eyes. There should be plenty of substance to the foreface, with a good depth from top to bottom. The muzzle is strong and long and, while tapering to the nose, it must not be carried to such an extreme as to give the appearance of being overshot. It must not show any weakness, be snipy or lippy. The lips must be tight fitting and clean. The nose must be black.

Eyes : The eyes are almond-shaped, as nearly as possible matching the surrounding coat, but darker rather than lighter in shade, and placed to look straight forward. They must not be in any way bulging or prominent, and must show a lively, alert and intelligent expression.

Ears : The ears should be of moderate size, but rather large than small, broad at the base and pointed at the tips, placed rather high on the skull and carried erect—all adding to the alert expression of the dog as a whole. (It should be noted in case novice breeders may be misled, that in Alsatian puppies the ears often hang until the age of six months and sometimes longer, becoming erect with the replacement of the milk teeth).

Mouth : The teeth should be strong and sound, gripping with a scissor—like action, the lower incisors just behind, but touching the upper.

Neck : The neck should be strong, fairly long with plenty of muscle, fitting gracefully into the body, joining the head without sharp angles and free from throatiness.

20

Forequarters : The shoulders should slope well back. The ideal being that a line drawn through the centre of the shoulderblade should form a right—angle with the humerus when the leg is perpendicular to the ground in stance. Upright shoulders are a major fault. They should show plenty of muscle, which is distinct from, and must not be confused with coarse or loaded bone, which is a fault. The shoulder—bone should be clean. The forelegs should be perfectly straight viewed from the front, but the pasterns should show a slight angle with the forearm when regarded from the side, too great an angle denotes weakness and while carrying plenty of bone, it should be of good quality. Anything approaching the massive bone of the Newfoundland, for example, being a decided fault.

Body : The body is muscular, the back is broadish and straight, strongly boned and well developed. The belly shows a waist without being tucked up. There should be a good depth of brisket or chest, the latter should not be too broad. The sides are flat compared to some breeds, and while the dog must not be barrel—ribbed, it must not be so flat as to be actually slab—sided. The Alsatian should be quick in movement and speedy but not like a Greyhound in body.

Hindquarters : The hindquarters should show breadth and strength, the loins being broad and strong, the rump rather long and sloping and the legs, when viewed from behind, must be quite straight, without any tendency to cow—hocks or bow—hocks which are both extremely serious faults. The stifles are well turned and the hocks strong and well let down. The ability to turn quickly is a necessary asset to the Alsatian, and this can only be there if there is a good length of thigh—bone and leg, and by the bending of the hock.

Feet : The feet should be round, the toes strong, slightly arched and held close together. The pads should be firm, the nails short and strong. Dewclaws are neither a fault nor a virtue, but should be removed from the hindlegs at four to five days old, as they are liable to spoil the gait.

Tail : When at rest the tail should hang in a slight curve, and reach at least as far as the hock. During movement and excitement it will be raised, but in no circumstances should the tail be carried past a vertical line drawn through the root.

Coat : The coat is smooth, but it is at the same time a double coat. The undercoat is woolly in texture, thick and close, and to it the animal owes its characteristic resistance to cold. The outer coat is also close, each hair straight, hard, and lying flat, so that it is rain—resisting. Under the body, to behind the legs, the coat is longer and forms near the thigh a mild form of breeching. On the head (including inside the ears), to the front of the legs and feet, the hair is short. Along the neck it is longer and thicker, and in winter approaches a form of ruff. A coat either too long or too short is a fault. As an average, the hairs on the back should be from 1 to 2 inches (25—50mm.) in length.

Colour : The colour of the Alsatian is in itself not important and has no effect on the character of the dog or on its fitness for work and should be a secondary consideration for that reason. All—white or near—white unless possessing black points is not desirable. The final colour of a young dog can only be ascertained when the outer coat has developed.

Weight and Size : The ideal height (measured to the highest point of the shoulder) is 22 to 24 inches (558—609mm.) for bitches and 24 to 26 inches (609—660mm.) for dogs. The proportion of length to height may vary between 10 : 9 and 10 : 8.5.

Faults : A long, narrow, Collie or Borzoi head. A pink or liver—coloured nose. Undershot or overshot mouth. Tail with curl or pronounced hook. The lack of heavy undercoat.

Reproduced by kind permission of the *Kennel Club*

The American Kennel Club Breed Standard

The following is the breed Standard by which the German Shepherd Dog is judged at American Kennel Club shows, as set down by the Board of Directors of the American Kennel Club on 9 April 1968 and published in the May 1968 issue of *Pure Bred Dogs   American Kennel Gazette*

The American Kennel Club's address is :

51 Madison Avenue.,
New York, N.Y.10010

Readers who require more specific information on the breed should contact the German Shepherd Dog of America, Inc. whose secretary is:

Miss B.L.Beisswenger,
17 West Ivy Lane,
Englewood, N.Jersey 07631
and whose delegate is:
Thomas L.Bennett,
137 Woodside Road,
Lancaster,
Philadelphia 17601

This Standard is based on the original 'S.V.' Standard. It was revised in 1943 and again in 1968.

General Appearance : The first impression of a good German Shepherd Dog is that of a strong, agile, well-muscled animal, alert and full of life. It is well balanced, with harmonious development of the forequarter and hindquarter. The dog is longer than tall, deep bodied, and presents an outline of smooth curves rather than angles. It looks substantial and not spindly, giving the impression, both at rest and in motion, of muscular fitness and nimbleness without any look of clumsiness or soft living. The ideal dog is stamped with a look of quality and nobility—difficult to define, but unmistakable when present. Secondary sex characteristics are strongly marked, and every animal gives a definite impression of masculinity or femininity, according to its sex.

Character : The breed has a distinct personality marked by direct and fearless, but not hostile, expression, self—confidence, and a certain aloofness that does not lend itself to immediate and indiscriminate friendships. The dog must be approachable, quietly standing its ground and showing confidence and willingness to meet overtures without itself making them. It is poised, but when the occasion demands, eager and alert; both fit and willing to serve in its capacity as companion, watch—dog, blind—leader, herding dog, or guardian, whichever the circumstances may demand. The dog must not be timid, shrinking behind its master or handler; it should not be nervous, looking about or upward with anxious expression or showing nervous reactions, such as tucking of tail to strange sounds or sights. Lack of confidence under any surroundings is not typical of good character. Any of the above deficiencies in character which indicate shyness must be penalized as very serious faults. It must be possible for the judge to observe the teeth and to determine that both testicles are descended. Any dog that attempts to bite the judge must be disqualified. The ideal dog is a working animal with an incorruptible character combined with body and gait suitable for the arduous work which constitutes its primary purpose.

Head : The head is noble, cleanly chiselled, strong without coarseness, but above all not fine and in proportion to the body. The head of the male is distinctly masculine, and that of the bitch distinctly feminine. The muzzle is long and strong with the lips firmly fitted, and its top line is parallel to the top line of the skull. Seen from the front, the forehead is only moderately arched, and the skull slopes into the long wedge-shaped muzzle without abrupt stop. Jaws are strongly developed. *Ears*—are moderately pointed, in proportion to the skull, open toward the front, and carried erect when at attention, the ideal carriage being one in which the centre lines of the ears, viewed from the front, are parallel to each other and perpendicular to the ground. A dog with cropped or hanging ears must be disqualified. *Eyes*—of medium size, almond-shaped, set a little obliquely and not protruding. The colour as dark as possible. The expression keen, intelligent, and composed. *Teeth*—42 in number—20 upper and 22 lower— are strongly developed and meet in a scissor bite, in which part of the inner surface of the upper incisors meet and engage part of the outer surface of the lower incisors. An overshot jaw or a level bite is undesirable. An undershot jaw is a disqualifying fault. Complete dentition is to be preferred. Any missing teeth, other than first premolars, is a serious fault.

Neck : The neck is strong and muscular, clean-cut and relatively long, proportionate in size to the head and without loose folds of skin. When the dog is at attention or excited, the head is raised and the neck carried high; otherwise typical carriage of the head is forward rather than up and little higher than the top of the shoulders, particularly in motion.

Forequarters : The shoulder blades are long and obliquely angled, laid on flat and not placed forward. The upper arm joins the shoulder blade at about a right angle. Both the upper arm and the shoulder blade are well muscled. The forelegs, viewed from all sides, are straight and the bone oval rather than round. The pasterns are strong and springy and angulated at approximately a 25 degree angle from the vertical.

Feet : The feet are short, compact, with toes well arched, pads thick and firm, nails short and dark. The dewclaws, if any, should be removed from the hindlegs. Dewclaws on the forelegs may be removed but are usually left on.

Proportion : The German Shepherd Dog is longer than tall, with the most desirable proportion as 10 to 8½. The desired height for males at the top of the highest point of the shoulder blade is 24 to 26 inches(609−660mm.); and for bitches 22 to 24 inches (558−609mm.). The length is measured from the point of the prosternum or breastbone to the rear edge of the pelvis, the ischial tuberosity.

Body : The whole structure of the body gives an impression of solidity without bulkiness. *Chest*—commencing at the prosternum, is well filled and carried well down between the legs. It is deep and capacious, never shallow, with ample room for lungs and heart, carried well forward, with the prosternum showing ahead of the shoulder in profile. *Ribs*—well sprung and long, neither barrel-shaped nor too flat, and carried down to a sternum which reaches to the elbows. Correct ribbing allows the elbows to move back freely when the dog is at a trot. Too round causes interference and throws the elbows out; too flat or too short causes pinched elbows. Ribbing is carried well back so that the loin is relatively short. *Abdomen*—firmly held and not paunchy. The bottom line is only moderately tucked up in the loin.

Top Line : *Withers*—the withers are higher than and sloping into the level back. *Back*—the back is straight, very strongly developed without sag or roach, and relatively short. The desirable long proportion is not derived from a long back, but from overall length with relation to height, which is achieved by length of forequarter and length of withers and hindquarter, viewed from the side. *Loin*—viewed from the top, broad and strong. Undue length between the last rib and the thigh, when viewed from the side, is undesirable. *Croup*—long and gradually sloping. *Tail*—bushy, with the last vertebra extended at least to the hock joint. It is set smoothly into the croup and low rather than high. At rest, the tail hangs in a slight curve like a sabre. A slight hook, sometimes carried to one side, is faulty only to the extent that it mars general appearance. When the dog is excited or in motion, the curve is accentuated and the tail raised, but it should never be curled forward beyond a vertical line. Tails too short, or with clumpy ends due to ankylosis, are serious faults. A dog with a docked tail must be disqualified.

Hindquarters : The whole assembly of the thigh viewed from the side is broad, with both upper and lower thigh well muscled, forming as nearly as possible a right angle. The upper thigh bone parallels the shoulder blade while the lower thigh bone parallels the upper arms. The metatarsus (the unit between the hock joint and the foot) is short, strong and tightly articulated.

Gait : A German Shepherd Dog is a trotting dog, and its structure has been developed to meet the requirements of its work. *General Impression* The gait is outreaching, elastic, seemingly without effort, smooth and rhythmic, covering the maximum amount of ground with the minimum number of steps. At a walk it covers a great deal of ground, with long stride of both hind legs and forelegs. At a trot the dog covers still more ground with even longer stride, and moves powerfully but easily, with co—ordination and balance so that the gait appears to be the steady motion of a well—lubricated machine. The feet travel close to the ground on both forward reach and backward push. In order to achieve ideal movement of this kind, there must be good muscular development and ligamentation. The hindquarters deliver, through the back, a powerful forward thrust which slightly lifts the whole animal and drives the body forward. Reaching far under, and passing the imprint left by the front foot, the hind foot takes hold of the ground; then hock, stifle and upper thigh come into play and sweep back, the stroke of the hind leg finishing with the foot still close to the ground in a smooth follow through. The over—reach of the hindquarter usually necessitates one hind foot passing outside and the other hind foot passing inside the track of the forefeet, and such action is not faulty unless the locomotion is crabwise with the dog's body sideways out of the normal straight line. *Transmission* The typical smooth, flowing gait is maintained with great strength and firmness of back. The whole effort of the hindquarter is transmitted to the forequarter through the loin, back and withers. At full trot, the back must remain firm and level without sway, roll, whip or roach. Unlevel topline with withers lower than the hip is a fault. To compensate for the forward motion imparted by the hindquarters the shoulder should open to its full extent. The forelegs should reach out close to the ground in a long stride in harmony with that of the hindquarters. The dog does not track on widely separated parallel

26

lines, but brings the feet inward toward the middle line of the body when trotting in order to maintain balance. The feet track closely but do not strike, nor cross over. Viewed from the front, the front legs function from the shoulder joint to the pad in a straight line. Viewed from the rear, the hind legs function from the hip joint to the pad in a straight line. Faults of gait, whether from front, rear or side, are to be considered serious faults.

Colour : The German Shepherd Dog varies in colour, and most colours are permissible. Strong rich colours are preferred. Nose black. Pale, washed out colours and blues and livers are serious faults. A white dog or a dog with a nose that is not predominantly black must be disqualified.

Coat : The ideal dog has a double coat of medium length. The outer coat should be as dense as possible, hair straight, harsh and lying close to the body. A slightly wavy outer coat, often of wiry texture, is permissible. The head, including the inner ear and foreface, and the legs and paws are covered with short hair, and the neck with longer and thicker hair. The rear of the forelegs and hind legs has somewhat longer hair extending to the pastern and hock, respectively. Faults in coat include soft, silky, too long outer coat, woolly, curly, and open coat.

Reproduced by kind permission of the *American Kennel Club*

Flamboyant of Monteray
owned by Miss J.Pratt
& Mr J.Wilson
(Photo: Diane Pearce)

27

The German Breed Standard

Reproduced below is the current Standard of the breed as used in Europe. It differs very little from the original Standard published by the S.V.(*Der Verein für Deutsche Schäferhunde*) in 1899. This Standard was added to in 1901 and 1909, slightly amended in 1920 and 1921 and again in recent years. This is a 1973 publication No.166 ex the FCI and the English translation is supplied by their always helpful office. Attesting its authenticity reads a footnote in German:

'Dieser, in englisher Sprache abgefasste Rassestandard ist vom Verein für deutsche Schäferhunde (SV) im VDH überprüft. Er stimmt mit dem Wortlaut des Rasse standards, herausgegeben vom SV in deutscher Sprache, überein'

The translation is dated, 8th February 1973

General Appearance: The German Shepherd Dog is a medium−large dog. The height at the withers is about 60cm. This height is established by taking a perpendicular line from the top of the shoulder blade, touching one elbow, to the ground with the coat parted or pushed down. The ideal height for the German Shepherd Dog as a working dog is 60−65cm for the dogs and 55−60cm for the bitches. The working and breeding value of dogs above or below the indicated heights is proportionately less. The German Shepherd Dog is slightly long, strong and well muscled. His bones are dry and their composition is firm. The German Shepherd is a trotting dog and his structure has been developed to best meet these requirements. That is to say, a long effortless trot which shall cover the maximum amount of ground with the minimum number of steps. The proper body proportion, firmness of back and muscles and the proper angulation of the forequarters and hindquarters serve this end. A harmonious appearance is desirable; however, the workability and trainability of the German Shepherd Dog are the most important factors. Secondary sex characteristics should be strongly marked and every animal should give a definite impression of masculinity or femininity, according to sex.

The first impression of a good German Shepherd Dog, according to the breed

Standard, is that of a strong, agile and intelligent animal which is well balanced and harmonious. By the way the dog moves and acts, it must be evident that a sound mind lives in a sound body, thus meeting the prerequisites of greatest endurance and being ready to perform his work at all times. Exhibiting exuberant temperament, he must be easy to handle, adaptable to every situation, and always willing and able to carry out his assigned duties. He must show courage and strength when it is necessary to defend his master or his master's property, he must also be willing to attack if his master so commands; however, on the other hand, he must be an attentive and pleasant house companion, friendly toward the family and familiar surroundings, especially to children and other animals and approachable by harmless strangers. All in all he should be stamped with a look of quality, nobility and respect-demanding self assurance.

Angulation and Gait : The German Shepherd is a trotting dog. His gait, the movement of his front and hind legs, is in diagonal sequence. Therefore, his forequarters and hindquarters must be angulated in such a way to allow him to propel himself forward by a long step of the hindquarters and compensating for this stride by a long step of the forequarters, without change in the top line. With the right proportion of length to height and respective length of bones, the dog has a far-reaching gait, travelling close to the ground, seemingly effortlessly, the head stretched forward, the tail slightly raised, showing a soft curved line from the tip of the ear over the neck and the back to the end of the tail.

Temperament and Character : Good nerves, attentiveness, willingness to guard, faithfulness, courage, aggressiveness, (willingness to accept overtures yet not willing to make them) are the most pronounced characteristics of a pure-bred German Shepherd Dog; fit and willing to serve in any capacity of companion, utility dog, watch dog, guard dog, sentry dog; leader of the blind and herding dog.

Forehead : Viewed from the side and front, moderately arched, without or just a slight centre indentation.

Cheeks : The cheeks are slightly rounded and not protruding. Viewed from above, the upper part of the head tapers slightly from the ears towards the nose, forming a soft dip at the forehead and tapers wedge–like to the muzzle.

Muzzle : The muzzle is strong.

Flews : The flews are tight, dry, lips firmly fitted. The ridge of the muzzle is nearly parallel to the extension line of the forehead.

Teeth : Very strong with the incisors fitting in a scissor–bite; neither over – nor undershot.

Ears : The ears are of medium size, broad at the base, high set, erect, pointed, and directed towards the front. Soft ears are undesirable; cut ears and hanging ears are disqualifying. Puppies often have hanging ears until the age of 4–6 months, sometimes even longer.

Eyes : The eyes are of medium size, almond-shaped, set a little obliquely and not protruding. Colour as dark as possible. Lively, intelligent expression.

Neck : Strong and muscular, of medium length, without loose skin or dewlap. When the dog is at attention or excited, the head is raised and the neck carried high, otherwise the typical carriage of the head is forward rather than up.

Body : Deep chest, however, not too broad; ribs well sprung neither barrel-shaped nor too flat. Abdomen firmly held and moderately tucked up. The back including the loin straight and strong; not too long between withers and croup. The body length should exceed the dog's height at the withers. Square and over-built dogs are highly undesirable. Loins broad and strong. Croup long and gradually sloping.

Tail : Bushy, reaching to the hocks; even though undesirable occasionally forming a hook. At rest the tail hangs in a slight curve like a sabre. When the dog is excited or in motion, the curve is accentuated and the tail raised; however, it should never be lifted beyond a line at right angle with the line of the back. The tail therefore, should not be carried straight up or curled (ring tail). Docked tails are disqualifying.

Forequarters : The shoulder blades should be long, laid on flat against the body and sloping well forward; not loaded. They join the upper arms at an approximate right angle. The forequarters must be well muscled. The legs, viewed from all sides, must be straight. The pastern firm, but not too steep (30 degrees angle). The elbows neither turned out nor turned in.

30

Hindquarters : Thighs broad and well muscled. The upper thigh bone (femur) slanted in relation to the respectively long stifle (tibia/fibula). The hock joint as well as the hocks (metacarpus) strong and firm.

Feet/Paws : Round, short, compact and toes well arched. Soles must be very hard. Nails short, strong, and dark. Occasionally dew claws may be found on puppies. Because these cause a broad movement and possibly injury to the hindquarters, they must be removed shortly after whelping.

Colour : Black, steelgrey, ashgrey, either solid coloured or with regular brown (tan), to yellow, to steelgrey markings; also a black saddle, dark clouded (indication of black or grey or lightbrown base with respective lighter markings); the so-called wolf-colour, the original colour of the wild dog. Small white markings on the chest are permissible. The undercoat is always lighter, except on black dogs. On a puppy, the final coat colour of the dog can only be determined after the outer coat is fully developed.

Hair
The Stockhaarige (Dense, Harsh Coat) German Shepherd Dog
The outer coat is dense, the individual hair is straight, firm, lies flat. The hair is short on the head of the dog, including the inner part of the ear, front of the legs, feet and toes; it is longer and denser at the neck. On the hindquarters, the hair is longer down to the hocks; on the thighs it is full. The length of the coat differs in various dogs; because of the different lengths of hair, different types of coat may be found. Too short, gopher—like hair is a fault.

The Long Stockhaarige (Dense, Harsh Coat) German Shepherd Dog
The individual hairs are longer, not always flat against the body. Especially, the hair is longer at the inner ear, behind the ears, and at the back side of the hindquarters; occasionally feathering between the knee and the hock joint; feathering at the ears. On the thighs the coat is long and dense. The tail is bushy and feathered. Due to the fact that this type of coat is not a weather—conditioned coat as the normal coat, it is not desirable; however, with sufficient undercoat, dogs of this coat type may still be used for breeding.

The Long—haired German Shepherd Dog

The hair is considerably longer than that of the 'Long Stockhaar' (see above) and usually parts on the back. An undercoat is only found in the area of the loins or is completely non—existent. The long—haired German Shepherd Dogs are usually narrow chested and have extremely pointed muzzles. Since the weather—conditioning and workability of the long—haired German Shepherd Dog is extremely reduced, they may not be used for breeding.

Faults : All faults reducing the use, endurance and working capability. Missing or weak sex characteristics (i.e.bitchy dogs or doggy bitches). Temperament faults contrary to the desired Shepherd Dog characteristics; lackadaisical, highly excitable, shy dogs, monorchids, cryptorchids (disqualification for showing and breeding), weak or flabby constitution, deficiency of bone or body substance and lack of firmness. Washed out colours, albinos (without any pigmentation and red nose), as well as white dogs (that means almost white to completely white dogs with black nose) may not be used for breeding and will be disqualified at a conformation show or trial. Furthermore, over or under sized dogs, badly structured or proportioned, dogs which are higher than long, too light or too heavy, faulty back, lack of angulation, as well as all faults negatively influencing the desired far-reaching trot and endurance; furthermore, overly short, weak, pointed or long muzzle; over or undershot, and other dentition faults, especially weak, discoloured or distemper teeth. Finally overly soft coat, too short or too long without undercoat; hanging or continuously badly carried ears; curled or ring-tail, badly carried tail, cropped ears and docked tail, as well as dogs whelped with short or stumpy tails.

Reproduced by kind permission of the *Federation Cynologique Internationale*

Comments on The Breed Standard

No two people will read and 'understand' the Standard in an identical way. It is best to treat it as a kind of blueprint describing the perfect German Shepherd Dog. That anyone has ever seen such a paragon remains improbable. Even the best dogs in the breed (or in any breed for that matter) are unlikely to reach a standard 'worth—level' of 75 percent. This suggests that there remains plenty of scope for improvement in German Shepherd Dogs if one is to attain sheer perfection.

In all breeds, there exist faddists who seek specific and preferred points to develop in their strains. Size, of course, has always been a desideratum, as is rear angulation, but if these are bred for and developed regardless of other points, more or just as vital, especially ones of temperament, then the system of breeding must be badly conceived. Exaggeration is bad too; beware of the breeder who tries to shape the Standard to fit his dog rather than the reverse.

Let us therefore consider the various points of the breed Standard.

Type : Type is difficult to define, but basically it comprises the quality and appearance essential in a dog if he is to epitomize the ideal model of his breed based on the description given in the Standard. You can usually recognize good type when you see it, but it often happens that some very typey dogs are unsound. You can have a dog with all the components of his body thoroughly well typed so that whilst standing he makes the 'perfect picture'. But get that same dog to move and it becomes clear at once that although the component parts are perfect they are not fused together in a proper and pleasing fashion. The dog is in effect unsound, and because he is unsound he immediately becomes suspect as a breeding proposition. The linkage between his parts are faulty, that is, no one part is joined soundly and effectively to another. His head might be ideal, his body too, yet the head is associated with the body by a neck (probably good as necks go) in an untidy, somehow irrelevant manner. His hindquarters, although well made, well muscled, and nicely angulated, go down to feet which, given the loose way they link, might belong to another German Shepherd Dog altogether! It is this lack of physical integration that is unsoundness—worse, it is transmittable in breeding. Such dogs are invariably quite useless to the serious breeder. Though a perfect picture whilst standing, when moved such a German Shepherd Dog is clearly an unsound animal. This shows just how important it is to see a dog in action before commenting on its worth. In effect, type must be complemented by complete soundness. Satisfaction rests somewhere between the two necessities; the degree can vary enormously depending on the specimen under review. Quite simply, it is controlled by the worth of his respective physical points as applied to the GSD breed Standard.

Temperament : The breed is noted for its brains and its sagacity is probably greater than that of any other breed. The German Shepherd Dog is friendly with people, including children, and other animals but never goes out of his way to importune. His main characteristics are loyalty, awareness, and fidelity. He is an active dog and ever ready to enter situations in a friendly yet determined manner. His outlook or expression is eager and intelligent.

General Appearance : The true German Shepherd Dog is at once handsome and imposing. He should show strength, suppleness, speed, and agility. There is at least a touch of majesty in his make−up, and he must give the appearance of being able to cope with trouble if the need arises. His record for superior work in the field of active service training is well known and puts him in a class well above other canines. This courage and determination should show on the face and in the movement of the real German Shepherd. Overall, he must be balanced, with no exaggerations, and his action must indicate absolute soundness.

Gait : The typical gait or action of the German Shepherd is unique. Exaggerated angulation of the hind limbs will render the movement faulty, as will upright shoulder emplacement. The gait should be a supple, flowing one and should cover plenty of ground, the hindlimbs propelling the body forward strongly and directly with no undulation. Inferior action comes from many features themselves inferior; these include bad angulation both fore and aft and also short backs, over−long or short legs, extension of hock, even thin pads. Some handlers do much to ruin an exhibit's true action in the ring. Once spoiled, it is not always easy to get a dog's movement back to normal.

Thus if a German Shepherd Dog is not made correctly in respect of his body, foreparts, hindparts, and feet, even his tail, which may be used as a kind of rudder when at speed or turning, he will not move in a manner typical of his breed. So if a dog fails in action, assuming he is neither tired (and GSD's are noted for their stamina), nor temporarily unsound (perhaps after an accident) then he must have some fault or imperfection in his structure and/or nervous system.

Bone : In a working breed required at times to cover long distances and engage in heavy duties, strong bone is a comitant of its make−up. The bone we are most concerned with in this instance is that of the legs, i.e. the forelegs and the hocks. It should not be round, as some people appear to think, but rather ovoid in form, firm and very strong as befits a breed that on occasions is involved in apprehending criminals. The Germans refer to GSD bone as 'trocken' (dry), a word which dispenses entirely with any suggestion of weakness and emphasizes strength and quality. Good bone structure contributes to elegance and classical outline, as well as to good deportment.

Back : The German Shepherd Dog's back should be fairly but not too short, a long back indicates inherent weakness. There is great strength and power in the dog's frame, which takes the bulk of its body shape from the length and formation of the dorsal spine and the typified firm broadness of the loins. The dorsal vertebrae is composed of thirteen connected bony segments, from each of which come a pair of ribs; nine of these extend downwards to join the sternum or breastbone. These are termed 'true' ribs. The remaining four are not so attached. The last rib is called a 'false' or floating rib.

The rib cage houses and protects the dog's heart and lungs and the major blood vessels are dispersed from here to the rest of the body. The lungs function in conjunction with the ribs — in effect, when the dog takes a breath of air, the diaphragm expands, rotates the ribs, and sucks air into the lungs. Thus the larger the chest the more lung room it will afford. The German Shepherd Dog's ribs should have a certain spring but should not be barrelled. They should be deep and go well back and be rather flat but not slabsided as such. The top line should slope gently from the withers to the croup and should be firm, straight, and strong.

Coat : The form of the German Shepherd's coat should be double. The top 'guard' should be strong and harsh in texture and highly protective against the elements, while the undercoat should be soft and woolly. Coats which are untypical, soft and silky ones for example, are useless to a working breed and are specially penalized in Europe. True coat texture is easily lost through casual breeding.

Tail : The tail is one of the German Shepherd's crowning glories ! No dog can be considered highly unless he can boast a fine tail, thickly furnished with rich fur. When at rest it hangs down in a slight curve, reaching at least to the point of hock. At one time in Germany the tail was allowed to repose turned slightly to one side in a curve. This is no longer approved, and today the tail must hang straight down with a slight curve when at rest and must be carried raised (but never above the level of the back) when the dog is in action.

Hindquarters : The topline should slope gradually to the croup, which in turn should slope down to the set—on of the tail. Back—line and croup—line should fuse evenly and without any interruption visually, although some *slight* arching over the loin may be apparent. The exact low degree of arching together with the firm musculation of the belly line must be maintained not only for their contribution to the dog's functioning at work, but also so as to earn points for general appearance. Arguments over rear angulation have beset the breed over past years. To some extent it has reached faddist proportions, and some GSD pundits consider that it is now so exaggerated that remedial rectification is required. When one examines many pictures from the early days and compares them with those of modern dogs, it is obvious that angulation of the hind limbs has been radically accentuated. Unfortunately, over–angulation has proved to be of no particular advantage to the breed. Stamina in the working dog is reduced and aesthetic appeal is lowered in the show dog, for both balance and gait are adversely affected.

Thighs : The thighs should be well muscled and strong. Muscle development should be long and supple, for this form of muscling is 'lasting' and permits great stamina. Bunched or 'bossy' muscles, although very strong, tire easily and do not lend themselves to the lithe, easy action expected of the German Shepherd Dog. Both thighs must be well padded with cartilage and ligaments, able to withstand the considerable stress put upon them by the dog in action. Ligaments will sometimes stretch, and if the resultant condition is ignored by the owner the effect can become chronic. The hock bone should be straight and strong. 'Cow hocks', that is when the points of hocks bend in towards each other, thereby throwing the feet out, are faulty. 'Bow hocks' – when the hock points turn away from each other, causing the feet to turn in, a condition known as 'in–toed' or 'pin–toed' are equally bad. If a dog has dew claws (rudimentary fifth digits) on the insides of his hindlegs, they should be removed soon after birth as they are inclined to make a dog move wide as he goes away.

Forequarters : The front aspect of the German Shepherd should be of straightness, good musculature without 'bossiness', and smooth clean lines from neck down to forelegs. The bone of the forelegs should be straight and clean. The whole should be positive. The foreparts take most of the weight of the dog when he is moving at speed, and the forelegs and forefeet steer him. Therefore the articulation between the lower end of the scapula (shoulder blade) and the upper end of the humerus (arm bone) should be so angled as to form a sort of shock–absorber against the jarring impact which a dog is subject to, especially at the gallop. The part below the knee including the pasterns should be strong and have ample spring.

It is very important for a GSD to have correct angulation between shoulder blade and upper arm; and an angle of 90 degrees is normally preferred. This results in greater stride and speed. Upright shoulders induce a stilted even mincing gait which is quite alien to the German Shepherd. The forelegs should travel well back below the body while maintaining the smooth flowing action required in the breed.

Chest : The GSD's chest should be deep, but not overly so, or good action will be lost. Overdevelopment of the forechest creates a bad 'fiddle' effect and impairs balance. False depth is sometimes produced by breeders seeking deeper 'keels'. This is a bad feature unless true depth can be incorporated by breeding in longer ribs to give greater breathing space.

Feet : The feet are very important as they are used for both steering and braking. They should be compact, since well–knit feet will serve a German Shepherd well in the field, providing the pads are nice and thick and the claws short and strong. A young dog should always be exercised on hard ground, preferably on cinder tracks. This will keep the feet well toned. Flat and splayed feet are heavily penalized in this breed. The pastern, which is equivalent to the wrist in man, lies below the knee joint in the lower part of the leg. When viewed from the side it should slope at an angle of about 30 degrees. Viewed from the front, the line of forelegs and feet is a straight one.

Head : In many breeds there is often a tendency to exaggerate the head; this is wrong if only because it falls into the category of a fad. However, in the German Shepherd Dog, the head is not the 'hallmark' of the breed and does not play a particularly important part, in contrast with Bull breeds for instance. Most important is that in the GSD the size of its head should be correct and proportionate to the overall balance of the dog. Ensure also that a dog's head is masculine and a bitch's feminine in cast and cut. A male's head should be bold in line and with some degree of arrogance in its mould. A female, on the other hand, should be more refined, her lines of head a little softer. You should be able to recognize the sex of any specimen by a mere glance at its head. The stop should be very slight; the muzzle required is a strong, wedge–shaped one, with very powerfully constructed jaw muscles. The lips should be clean and tight. It is a bad fault if any impression of the Collie is given. The ears must be medium size; small ears are untypical and give an alien aspect to the dog; big ears are ugly and suggest some deficiency in breeding. Drop ears are of course quite beyond the pale, and in fact any ears which tend to spoil the true line of head are faulty. The same applies to the carriage of ears and their set–on.

Neck : The outline of the neck's crest must be strong and relatively long with a firm, graceful, muscular curve; no dewlap should be shown. The crest is made up of even segments of the cervical vertebrae, running in an upward and bending line from rather low down between the shoulder blades (joining the dorsal vertebrae) to a point just at the rear of the dog's skull. The neck needs considerable thrust and power to administer the head. A neck that is too short will lack resilience; one that is too long lacks striking power. When the German Shepherd Dog is alert and excited, the head is raised and the neck held high, but the normal head carriage is forward rather than high. When the dog is in action the head is raised a little higher than the shoulders. A good neck contributes greatly to a dog's general appearance; it should fuse imperceptibly into the body via the withers.

Eyes : The true German Shepherd Dog eye should be almond–shaped and set rather obliquely. Most dogs lacking in correct breed outlook usually have their eyes set wrongly in their head; possibly they are too small, maybe too large or wrong in colour. The GSD's eye should be a soft dark brown and set to look straight ahead with a keen, intelligent expression. A 'varminty' expression is quite wrong, this is more suitable for the little earth–entering Terrier. Eyes which are too light in colour tend to spoil expression. The German Shepherd's eyes can bear some relation to the colour of the surrounding coat, but nevertheless eyes which are very light suggest shrewdness rather than intelligence, which is not what the breeder wants to cultivate; indifferent expression can sometimes arise from bad health. Eyes which are too deep set destroy expression, and bulging eyes give a vapid appearance. All these things militate against good general appearance in the show ring and effect the ability of the working dog in service.

Dentition : The topic of mouths has produced a great deal of acrimony in many breeds, and the German Shepherd is no exception. The Standard describes what we know as the level mouth. This gives a scissor bite, that is, one with the upper incisors resting over an upon the incisors of the lower jaw with no apparent space between them. The objectionable 'over–shot' jaw, in which the incisors of the upper jaw protrude beyond those of the lower jaw with a noticeable space between them is a bad fault, as is the decadent 'under–shot' mouth in which the incisors of the lower jaw project beyond those of the upper jaw, as in the Bulldog. German Shepherd Dog enthusiasts attach considerable significance to premolars, because anything less than a normal permanent dental formula suggests a hereditary deficiency, a situation against which any self respecting breeder needs to guard.

The adult dog should have the following quota of teeth:

38

	Upper Jaw	Lower Jaw
Cutting Teeth (Incisors)	6	6
Tusks or Eye Teeth (Canines)	2	2
(Pre-molars)	8	8
Grinding Teeth (Molars)	4	6

German Shepherds are not the only dogs which experience occasional shortages in the number of premolars produced. The condition is fairly common in other long—headed breeds and may well have nothing to do with progressive hereditary deficiency, probably resulting from unwise selective breeding by some owners. Whatever the reason, the matter is viewed with seriousness by the Germans in particular, though the British and Americans seem less concerned. The reason for preferring the level mouth is that it allows for a clean, holding bite. The over—shot mouth is a weak one and is often associated with a snipey foreface, although in its moderate form it will escape the notice of a show judge. A distinct under—shot jaw is a serious fault since it handicaps a dog when he takes hold, his bite being bruising rather than cutting. Even worse than this are the 'flush' mouth (sometimes referred to as the 'dead—level' or more confusingly as the 'even' mouth) and the 'wry' mouth. In the 'flush' mouth the tips of the upper and the lower incisors meet spot—on without intermeshing; and in the 'even' mouth the two sets of incisors meet cross—wise. Neither mouth can bite through anything. Worse, the dentition becomes cracked after a few years through constant abrasion.

Colour : It is sometimes said of dogs that 'no good dog is a bad colour'. Be this as it may, certain rules have to be followed in breeding, and it was discovered many years ago that some colours do no good to a breed. Black—and—tans were ostracized in Bulldogs, because, had they been allowed to procreate, those colour markings would have spread through the breed like lightning and introduced other coat colours of displeasing hues in their wake. If allowed too much rein, in a breeding programme whites would soon 'take over', producing whites and parti-colours in abundance. The best rule in breeding in dogs is to keep to dark pigmentations as this will help to keep the pale and paling colours away. Pale and insipid colours are anathema to any breed and, although it may seem hard to penalize a good dog with a dilute coloured coat, it is really asking for trouble to put him in the cards. When you place a dog in the prizes you are in effect telling breeders to use him. Those who follow your advice may repent so doing. Details of the technicalities of colour and colour breeding are beyond the scope of this book. For these it is best to turn to books specially prepared and written by expert geneticists; specially relevant to the German Shepherd Dog is M.B. Willis' *The German Shepherd Dog, Its History, Development and Genetics*, published by K. & R. Books (UK) & Arco USA 1977.

Soundness : Soundness can be defined as the ability of the dog to do his job properly, with the entire physical support of his body as well as of his mind, as such it is really the most important aspect of the dog. Unsoundness can be inherited or aquired. Anatomical unsoundness can be seen in skeletal faults such as upright shoulders, invariably an inherited defect. Cow—hocks can be inherited too, but they can come about if a dog is badly reared in puppyhood or kept in some unfavourable environment. Of course, a dog imbued with certain genetic faults may well pass these on to his progeny, and they will do the same to their offspring in turn. On the other hand, an animal with induced or aquired features of unsoundness will not pass them on. Every part of a dog's body should be able to work *soundly* and in unison to an effective end, which means perfection in movement and posture. However, both in work and when he is judged for show, a dog is assessed on the way he is affected on the day in question. By this rule alone he must be judged. Soundness of temperament is even more important. A vicious or untenable dog or one that lacks breed character can be considered unsound.

Faults : Faults are indicated in all three Standards, the different countries involved place varying degrees of importance on them.

Ch.Shootersway Brangaina

40

CHAPTER 3

Breeding

Most people who own a handsome German Shepherd Dog will be tempted at some time or other to try their hand at reproducing his or her kind. The breed excites tremendous admiration so the sales potential is high.

A breeder's aim is to produce a German Shepherd Dog which is at least as good as the one he owns, better if possible. If he can achieve the latter then he will have done a worthwhile service to his breed and will obtain for himself the real sense of satisfaction that comes from breeding a good specimen. Sadly, few breeders possess what can be claimed as a sound working knowledge of genetics, though oddly enough many dog–lovers do have what can be termed 'an eye' for a dog. This instinct has held many in good stead in their careers and enabled them to produce, by good assessment of mating pairs, some worthwhile stock.

First of all look at your bitch. Is she good ? Has she turned out as well as you expected ? What have the experts said about her ? Has she a good pedigree, a good strain ? If you are a lucky owner then you can answer 'yes' to most of these questions and feel heartened that, having picked the right dog for her, you at least stand a fairly good chance of breeding something nice from her. If she is just an average specimen with a fair share of faults and not from the pre–eminent bloodline in her breed, then your task is perhaps more difficult, but at least you have the right to try to improve upon her by careful selection of her mate. Providing you have a reasonably good bitch who is sound both physically and temperamentally, never be persuaded to delay trying your hand at breeding. Too many people with a flair for breeding good dogs have been kept in the background by others in the fancy who have told them not to breed because their bitch was 'not good enough'. An *average* bitch with type is good enough to breed from providing you intend to improve upon her. The only ones to keep free from puppies are the vicious and unsound. Bad mothers are also a nuisance, but one can seldom find out their shortcomings without giving them a litter first, even though this vicissitude runs in families of bitches; this will at least forewarn you and allow you to take precautionary measures to protect the puppies and your interests.

If you plan to breed German Shepherd dogs regularly, as opposed to a single venture with just one bitch, then you must steel yourself to keeping only good bitches in your kennel. This does not refer to the old and much–loved animal who has been in the home for many years and is part and parcel of the family. A pal of this kind deserves and indeed should have every care and comfort that you can bestow upon her. My comment refers to the *passé* breeding stock which sometimes accumulates in the kennel, serving no useful purpose and merely creating expense. You can serve such an animal better by finding it a good home somewhere. There it will receive individual attention (which you may be unable to provide) and become a pet in its own right with a nice family. This is better for it than to let it finish its days in a kennel, enjoying human companionship only for brief periods.

The Pedigree

To many people the dog's pedigree is a mere piece of paper. They take it home when they buy their dog, put it in a safe place somewhere, and promptly forget about it. To you as a breeder, however, it is an important document. Remember though that a dog is only as good as its pedigree and, no matter how superb and handsome it is to look at, if it has some poor ancestry in the blood this will fashion the shape and quality of her stock issue. Conversely, no pedigree is worth any more than the dog it refers to. You might have a pedigree before you brimful of champions – the best in the breed. It will mean very little if your German Shepherd is a poor specimen! The ideal is to own a good–looking dog with a good–looking pedigree. From such a dog or bitch you stand a very reasonable chance of producing good puppies.

It is important to study your bitch's pedigree. What has she behind her? Do her ancestors boast the prestige of a noted strain or are they mediocre in form and lacking note? Try to obtain the help of a person well steeped in German Shepherd lore and modern breed history. He or she should know the dogs of the past twenty years and will probably have judged most of them or at least have watched them being judged from the ringside. He is sure to recollect their stamp, remember their careers, their colours, size, and reputations. He will also remember their faults. It is odd how experts, even the unbiased ones, recall faults more easily than good points. But you will want to know both and you must press for information on the dogs whose names appear on the piece of paper in front of you. If one man cannot supply enough, ask others, but refer only to people with good reputations themselves — people who can impart facts

Ch.Rossfort Rissalma
owned by Mrs M.Hunter
(Photo: Diane Pearce)

Ch.Archduke of Rozavel
owned by
Mrs Thelma Gray
(Photo: Diane Pearce)

43

which are authentic, not mere quesswork or heresay.

Draft out your pedigree on a large piece of paper, and beneath the name of every dog and bitch ancestor write in its own square the data you have gleaned. Try to get details on *every* animal, even if this entails writing to people long since out of the breed. You will often find someone in their family who recalls the dog that their sister, brother, or father owned and can tell you something useful about it. But do not forget to enclose a stamped addressed envelope. From the facts you accumulate you should be able to form a perfect word picture of the ancestral qualities and faults behind your bitch, probably sufficient to ensure that when you come to select a stud dog for her you will at least be forearmed with knowledge which will enable you to avoid in her puppies any duplication of her faults capable of being passed on in double measure to her progeny.

Pedigrees can usually be relied upon these days. In the very old days of all breeds, and German Shepherd Dogs were no exception, records of a dog's breeding were kept casually, to say the least. In certain cases, information was jealously guarded by both owners and breeders, especially if the specimens involved were good ones. The pedigree was then thought of as a 'secret formula' which provided a good specimen than as what we now know it to be; a breeding record to be used freely in an effort to improve subsequent generations.

Breeding Methods

Line–breeding
Line–breeding is the most popular system of breeding dogs today. It is quite simple, providing care is taken not to introduce stock which falls below Standard quality. Line–breeding is really the mating of relatives and entails the following crosses:

grandson to grand–dam

grandsire to grand–daughter

cousin to cousin

It includes the mating of aunts and nephews, uncles and nieces and half brothers and sisters. Briefly, it means that quite closely related animals can be mated but *not* immediate relatives such as brother and sister. This form of union falls into the category of in−breeding. Although in line−breeding the pedigree of both mates should carry similar bloodlines, it is not essential that they should all have the same bloodlines, and a common ancestor may well appear twice in the last five generations. When assessing the pedigrees of both the dam and her prospective mate, as you will do in due course, look for one or two strong, vital lines to a dominant sire or dam whose type and quality you wish to aim for in the litter to be bred. If these are present, it is sometimes a good thing if the remaining parts of the pedigrees are not involved with effective bloodlines capable of counteracting, perhaps adversely, the effect of an ancestral sire on whose type and characteristics you have set your sights. The method of line-breeding is sound, although you may well have to wait patiently for results, in contrast with in−breeding, which although faster is fraught with greater dangers. Line−breeding takes time to establish purity of strain and once this has been achieved, there is not much more that can be done while your own kennel stock is being employed in the programme of breeding. You will have to consider introducing fresh blood; though such a move has its hazards, with care you will be able to maintain the purity you have achieved in your strain and inject it with a new lease of life.

Mikorr Aquarius
owned by Mr M.Orr
(Photo: Diane Pearce)

In—breeding

In—breeding is the mating of closely—related dogs, that is, son to mother, father to daughter, brother to sister. It should be done only in lines that are very strong and which show a high standard of type, health, soundness, and temperament. That these characteristics need to be perpetuated with each and every generation goes without saying, and in—breeding will aid such dominance. Only really first—class material must be employed; and if you try in—breeding with lowly stock you will do no more than 'fix' lowly points in your strain. This point illustrates the aim of in—breeding — to secure firmly the *good* points in your strain. If however your strain is liberally endowed with a number of indifferent features, then it will establish some of these for you too! This is why only animals which fall into a category which can claim freedom from *distinct* defects can be permitted entry into such a breeding programme. Rigorous culling of unwanted stock must take place prior to the planned furtherance of each generation. The breeder must be honest with himself, recognize where weaknesses exist in his stock, and employ only parental pairs which he knows in his heart can maintain the high standard of his kennel. If he omits this assessment he will be doomed to failure, for the longer defects are permitted to exist the more time and effort will be needed to eradicate them, and there is always the very real possibility that degeneration will creep in to ruin the work of years.

Out—crossing

In serious dog breeding, the out—cross is seldom employed today. The system has its value when the out—cross employed is a dog which has some connection with the original strain, perhaps linked through a pre—potent line. In the old days, an out—cross was used to improve a deficiency which it was believed existed in a working strain. For example, a Bulldog was put to Greyhounds by Lord Orford because it was thought that the latter breed needed stamina, whether such a move proved worthwhile we do not know. The only out—cross system of any value is when an outside dog can improve the health and type of a strain which has deteriorated, perhaps because of slapdash breeding. Some folk believe that an out—cross dog can improve, invigorate, even produce big winners from a negative strain. This is not so, and if by chance such a big winner did arise from the strain it would be no more than 'sport', a good specimen but without anything worthwhile in its blood and probably incapable of passing on even mediocre qualities in his issue.

If an out—cross must be employed — this very often is the case in far flung districts where members of the breed are really sparse and the bitch owner has little or no choice — then at least make sure that both parents–to–be are sound and healthy in all respects before allowing any union to take place. If, however an out–cross is planned with a specific purpose in mind, then make sure that the dog has factors which render him at least competent to correct any in–bred faults which the bitch possesses. Remember that a sire endowed with such factors and thus able to rectify the fault is a much better agent as an out–cross than a dog with such strong and dominant bloodlines that he can completely submerge the fault yet cause to arise to the surface some bad unsuspected feature. In his out–cross results the breeder must be prepared for an uneven litter and may experience some disappointment at the apparent lack of success of the exercise. Very often the good points expected will appear in the second generation, the grandchildren, rather than in the initial progeny.

The Bitch

You now have to decide whether your own bitch (assuming you have one) is to be employed in your breeding programme or whether you intend to buy one. Many people believe that the female is the more important of a mating pair, at least as far as determining the quality of the puppies is concerned. It is an acknowledged fact that, whereas it is easier to assess a dog's abilities at stud by virtue of the greater number of offspring he produces, a bitch's progeny must necessarily be much fewer. Consider objectively therefore the female lines as far as possible, because tail–female (the dam's dam's dam — or family) is more important than tail–male (the sire's sire's sire — or line).

This means that you *must* have a good bitch if you are to breed really good puppies. It has already been pointed out that you are entitled to use any sound, healthy, and reasonably typical bitch for breeding in a fair effort to improve on her particular virtues through the medium of her puppies. However, if show stock is your intent, you will need to aim a little higher than a mediocre bitch as your producer. Obviously, with a good bitch you might breed some very good puppies with quite an ordinary stud dog, but even a successful sire may well fail to produce anything but ordinary stock from a plain bitch.

You should buy the best bitch you can afford. This does not mean that a bitch has to be expensive, but if you get the opportunity to purchase a young female of obvious worth at a fair price she may well repay you twentyfold. Seek an adult bitch of not more than twenty months or a well-grown puppy as free from faults in her type and construction as possible. Employ a knowledgeable companion to advise you or put your trust in a reputable German Shepherd Dog kennel of which there are a good number. Make sure you know the breed Standard before you start negotiating, and put in a lot of time at major shows (especially Championship events) where the breed is on display and being judged. Listen to the competent authorities talking about the exhibits and judging results. See whether you can follow their lines of thought for yourself. Make sure that the people you listen to know what they are talking about. Too many folk in dogs 'think' they know. Many years' experience in a breed such as the German Shepherd Dog qualifies *most* people to pontificate reliably on the dog, but a long time in the breed does not necessarily make an expert. Some enthusiasts can learn in five years what it takes others thirty years to assimilate. As in life, some do better and learn quicker than their colleagues. The person who really knows is usually a well–established person in the breed, perhaps a noted breeder, judge, or writer. Seek out such a figurehead and learn from him or her. Never expect to come by the information you want too easily, and certainly never take it without proffering thanks for it. It has probably taken your informant many years to come by and has been acquired over periods of stress and bitter disappointments, and this should be borne in mind.

Now that you know something of the breed you will commence your search. Have nothing to do with a bitch who is too small, shelly, and fine. Such a female is not equipped for the rigours of puppy breeding, quite apart from being untypical in appearance. A good German Shepherd bitch must have some

Ch.Shooterway Xanthos
of Colgay
owned by
Mr Colliers
(Photo: Diane Pearce)

48

substance, plenty of room inside, and a pelvis of adequate width. It is also important that she is quite feminine — a doggy bitch is objectionable. Check her teeth to ensure that she has a good, level mouth and that her dental condition is good, and that of the gums as well. Watch for signs of nervousness, but bear in mind that many young females are ill−at−ease in the company of strangers and what seems to be nervousness may be no more than acute suspicion of your presence. The matter should be followed up for your satisfaction, however, just as you should any other feature of your intended purchase which worries you. Take each 'worry' as it comes and eliminate them one by one, not only by judicious questioning but by physical handling of the subject until you are completely satisfied.

Ensure that the bitch is amply boned and carries great depth of rib and brisket. If you looked at her sideways, the depth should reach *at least* to a line passing through the point of the elbow. The great strength and suppleness of back in an Alsatian is of tremendous importance and is essential to the speed and versatility of action for which this breed is noted. Check her shoulders closely; their emplacement should be such that the scapula is well laid back thereby allowing good fore−action and providing for elegance and balance of the body's general structure. The hindquarters are made to propel the dog and the legs in particular must be very powerful; the second thigh must be well developed, and the stifle should be well angulated (bent) with nice strong hocks. Like the forelegs which need to be strong and straight to support the body weight in front, the hind limbs must be straight and clean and the pasterns firm without

Astan of Akir
owned by Mr & Mrs Yates
(Photo: Diane Pearce

49

any slackness.

The bitch *must* have a typical good German Shepherd head. Heads are important in all breeds; nevertheless a good brood bitch has to be chosen for *overall* virtues, and no one feature should outshine the others, especially to the point of exaggeration, which is a fault in itself ! The head should be of good length and the jaw should be very strongly made. Snipiness, that is, a shallow and pointed weak muzzle, is a bad fault. Femininity is of absolute importance, and coarseness and dogginess are characteristics to be despised in a bitch. Look at her eyes, although if her expression is true you can be reasonably confident that the eyes are right. They must be dark or match the colour of the surrounding coat — light eyes suggest shrewdness rather than intelligence and impart a somewhat alien expression. The correct shape of the German Shepherd Dog eye is almond. Round eyes give a staring, vapid look which is quite wrong. Deviation from any one of these required features will mar a Shepherd's true expression.

As far as colour is concerned, any conventional colour will do unless you have a personal preference. The coat itself is important in as much as a bitch with a 'naturally' poor coat will never prove a useful brood. The coat should be smooth, neither too long nor too short, but you should allow for the time of the year and for the fact that a German Shepherd bitch's moult is often quite profuse compared with a dog's. The tail should be well furnished and carried in the manner demanded by the Standard.

Be sure to get your prospect to stand so that you can walk round her assessing her balance and stance. Ensure good overall body linkage, that is, the way the

Eveleys Bonnie Prince
Charlie
owned by Mr C.Llewellyn
(Photo: Diane Pearce)

50

various parts couple, quarters to body, set−on of tail, neck to body, head to neck and so on. Seen from the side, the neck will reveal whether the head is held nobly as it should be, sometimes, when the shoulder formation is faulty,(i.e. too upright), the neck will be held too low and the head will be thrust forward rather than held high. Look at her feet; if they are too spread and flat she will not move well when you come to see her in action. In fact, it is an interesting and worthwhile exercise just before you see her in action to wager with yourself how you *think* she will move from what you have seen of her body features standing.

Finally, you *must* see the bitch in action. Matters should be so arranged that a competent handler moves her at varying speeds from a walk to a fast trot. Any deficiencies in her soundness should become apparent during these exercises, and you will then be in a position to confirm your decision. Stand at one end of the arena in which the bitch is to be moved and let her be taken directly away from you in a straight line. Remember, the German Shepherd's hindquarters are singularly adapted to take the dog off at speed, with a long−reaching gait which can re−direct the dog suddenly at will. However, since the dog is on a leash, she will be unable to show her entire repertoire of speed, and you will have to assess her hind action as you see it. This means that action or gait, as it is sometimes termed, should be 'straight and true'. The hind legs must go away well separated from the other, moving in their own track, the action being firm, positive, and sound. There must be no suggestion of 'toeing−in' or that the action is 'close−behind', a show term indicating that a dog's hind feet are kept together in movement closer than is correct. Another fault occurs when one

Ch.Ullswood Folly
owned by Mr W.A.Morris
(Photo: Diane Pearce)

hind leg is kicking out sideways; this suggests some structural weakness at the hip. Action *must* always be flowing and free.

The bitch should be brought towards you. The action in this case must be positive, the legs being picked up well and not 'paddled' or 'plaited', that is, when one arm is passed over or nearly over the other as the dog comes towards you. Smooth, graceful action in a dog or bitch is the only movement acceptable in the German Shepherd Dog world. The animal must not move with a short stride or a mincing up—and—down gait. The whole aspect of the German Shepherd should show movement which is long—reaching, positive, and highly effective when herding. Consequently, every muscle must contribute tellingly to the end result.

You have now given your bitch a pretty good overhauling. If she conforms to your requirements and has the personal approval of the expert you have brought with you, then buy her, for she should be right. Thank the vendor for being so patient and for acquiescing in your whims, and take home your investment.

The Dog

As the dog you are likely to use with your bitch will probably belong to someone else, you are free to take your time finding him, for you should have many dogs to choose from. *Never* use an untried dog at stud. You might fancy your chances as an assessor of canine virtues in the blood, but you will need to be little more than a magician to 'hit the jackpot' with such a sire. It is better to let someone else try him first — then you can look at his puppies (taking their dam into consideration) and judge better his propensities.

Always choose a stud dog on his record as a stud dog, for his progeny brand him as good or bad at the job. A show dog with all the card and ribbons a winner can muster in his brief term on the show bench should never influence you. Much of his winning can be worthless, taken in classes where the competition is sparse or mediocre. Many a champion has won his third and deciding Challenge Certificate at some out—of—the—way Championship Show which is invariably poorly supported by the usual show—going crowd. Plenty of first prizes are very nice, but they do not do much more than tell you that the dog is probably a good specimen in himself, a handsome one, no doubt; they do not tell you what good he can do to his breed. The 'good' that comes from a dog is what he can produce; by the value of a dog's progeny is his name made and impressed in the annals of his breed.

Do not think that because your bitch is deficient in one aspect or another that her fault or faults can be corrected at once by putting her to a dog who is strong in the features she lacks. The primary task is to make yourself aware of the weak points in her make—up . Unless you do this and freely accept her faults you will never correct them. Any fault can be bred out of a strain, given time, care, and prudent calculation. What you have to guard against is breeding in other faults hitherto unknown to the strain while attempting to disperse those you know about! So look for a dog who is a real German Shepherd. He must be handsome, upstanding, masculine, and quite typical and should certainly conform closely to the breed Standard. Find this kind of sire and then look around at the litters he has produced, preferably young sons and daughters of his who have reached the yearling stage. Assuming that they look good and that some are winning already in the show circuits, then you may have the dog you seek—provided of course that he lines up satisfactorily with your bitch in the very important matters of their respective breeding. Take *his* pedigree and do with it what you did with the bitch's—fill in the description of those of his ancestors about whom you can obtain data. Then, placing the dog's dossier above that of the bitch, compare them point by point, ancestor with ancestor. If line-breeding is to be the plan of your campaign, then you must find within at least the first four generations the name of a beautiful and noted German Shepherd Dog worth breeding to. His name should appear as a common denominator to both pedigrees.

Make absolutely certain that the stud dog possesses an ideal temperament. If he did most of his winning under judges who qualify as German Shepherd Dog specialists it is highly probable that he will be of the right disposition, for German Shepherd Dog people recognize the need to maintain temperament .

The Mating

Your bitch must be ready for taking on maternal duties; this means not only that she should be of reasonably mature physical proportions but also that she must be past her first 'heat' or season, therefore about fifteen months of age or older. You will presumably have a fairly good idea of when her next heat is due. It is best to advise the stud dog owner that you propose to use his dog; later, when she nears her time of season, give him adequate warning of the date. Once she begins to show 'colour': a bright blood discharge at the mouth of

Ch.Sadira Francine
owned by
R.J.& D.D.Winfrow
(Photo: Diane Pearce)

Ch.Kenmilsorans Girl
owned by Mrs G.Uglione
(Photo: Diane Pearce)

the vulva (which will have swollen a little a few days earlier followed by an intermediary pinkish secretion), then you will know that she will shortly be ready for mating. The term is usually between ten and fourteen days from the commencement of the initial discharge, by which time all signs of blood will have dispersed, although the actual oestrum or season itself usually lasts about three weeks.

Bitches vary enormously in their preferred day for mating. Some will receive a dog any time between the tenth and fourteenth day, even a little earlier or later, others seem to like more specific days. These have to be catered for or you will never get them mated; if you have to learn from experience that your bitch likes to be mated on, say, the eleventh day of her heat, then you must ensure that you book her for the stud dog for just that day – no other will do. Another type of bitch, and this kind is rather a nuisance, becomes ripe for mating over a very short span of time, sometimes only a few hours in their season. It is not always easy to catch them at this time; and the answer seems to be that both dog and bitch should be kennelled in adjoining runs. Then when the bitch is ready for the dog she will indicate this in the usual manner and the dog can be introduced at once. Such an arrangement is rather trying to the stud dog who will be 'teased' to his disadvantage perhaps for many hours before he can get to the bitch. Needless to add, not many stud dog owners care for bitches of this kind either, and if you have such a female you may find extra fees and or charges to pay for the inconvenience she causes at the visited kennel.

Hendrawens Charade of
Charavigne
owned by
Miss M. Hinds
(Photo: Diane Pearce)

55

It is usual for the bitch to visit the dog, although some stud dog owners do not mind doing it the other way round so long as you pay fares etc. Often enough it suits the bitch better to be mated on her own territory when the job can be accomplished with the minimum delay. However, if you take your charge to the dog, try to arrange for the union to be effected early in the morning. Always try to accompany your bitch to the dog. No bitch should be sent a long distance by train to arrive in strange surroundings and find herself involved with a dog whom she may well not like. Being in season she will most probably be in a very nervous state, and a bitch in a distressed frame of mind is liable to 'miss' even after a good mating. If this happens you will have to wait at least another six months before you can try again, quite apart from incurring extra expense. Furthermore if you are present at the scene of the mating you can come away feeling satisfied that the dog in use was the one of your choice and that you saw things through from start to finish.

Ensure that both animals have had a free run round with ample time to attend to their natural functions. If the stud dog is an experienced animal he will usually lose little time in making overtures. It is best to have both dogs on their respective leashes during the introductions; this will allow the bitch to be edged away from him if she grabs at him in annoyance. It may seem prudent to present her to him rear end first, when his attentions will soon excite her. If you and the stud dog owner feel that the pair will get on well together, they can be released and watched closely as they run free. Never leave a mating pair unattended. Some breeders seem to prefer a 'natural' mating. This entails leaving dog and bitch alone to conduct affairs unaided and in their own way. Sometimes the pair do effect copulation without much ado and, of course, if this happens it is ideal. However, more often than not there is a skirmish or two before the dog can enter the bitch, and even when entry has been effected and a 'tie' made a fidgety and impatient bitch can do a dog and herself a good deal of harm.

The stud dog's natural instinct will make him take the initiative and mount the bitch from behind. He will at once begin to thrust at her, and an experienced male will soon enter. Once this has been noted, the stud dog owner should come behind and steady the dog squarely and firmly against the bitch's rear while you should hold your bitch's head firmly by clasping each side of her neck. This will not only give her confidence and reassurance at your presence but will prevent her from swinging round at the crucial moment and trying to dislodge the dog. If matters proceed well a 'tie' will soon be achieved: this means that seminal fluid is being deposited and that a proper mating can be assumed. The 'tie' is caused by a bulb situated in the dog's penis which becomes engorged with blood as the penis erects and swells to several times its normal size. It is then held securely and firmly in place by the sphincter muscle of the bitch's vagina, thereby locking both animals together. If it can be accomplished, it is best to turn the pair tail−to−tail for their own comfort while the mating lasts. This can be achieved by lifting the dog carefully so that his forelegs are brought off the bitch's back and put on the ground beside her. Then take one of his hind legs and gently lift it over the bitch's back, at the same time swivelling him round and away from her. They will end up with their heads pointing different ways but will remain 'tied'.

Unions last from a few minutes up to as long as an hour and a half, although the usual time is twenty minutes. The mating pair should be watched until they come apart, as towards the end of the union one or other or both of them will begin to fidget. Once parted, the dog should be removed from the bitch's presence and his comfort attended to by ensuring that his sheath has returned to the correct position over the penis. The bitch should be dried over at the back, and both animals can then be allowed to drink: they should be fed, if necessary, a little later. Don't worry if you notice that seminal fluid appears to have been spilled. It is likely that much more spermatozoa than has been wasted will have been deposited in the bitch's vagina: remember that in one mating many million sperms are released so the chances of a 'miss' (failure to conceive) are slight. This presumes of course that all other factors are good and normal.

At this point, it is interesting to consider the tail−to−tail natural mating position of dogs (and other animals so provided for by nature). In the wild state, a mating pair with their biting jaws or armament at each end are in a position for strategic turning in a complete circle if they should be attacked at such an inconvenient time. They are therefore far less vulnerable than if both their backs were turned the same way.

Some breeders prefer to have their bitch mated twice by the stud dog. This seems to give them added confidence that the bitch will 'take' and prove successful in having puppies. With a stud dog in regular use this is quite unnecessary if the initial mating was a good one. With a dog never before used at stud, and elderly male, or one seldom used, it can be a good idea; in this case the second union should follow the first within twenty-hours. The idea behind this is that the second service will be stimulated by the first in the cases of the stud dogs just referred to. This is a dubious belief. Remember that most German Shepherd Dogs are virile and that things seldom go wrong if their mating is handled expertly. It is therefore a good idea to get a young stud dog 'shown the ropes' at say ten months of age by a matron bitch whose receptive manner at mating time will give him confidence. Once he has had a stud job, it is best to let him rest until he has a second bitch at say, fifteen months of age. Then from two years onwards he can start his stud career in earnest. But, keep a close eye on him to ensure that he maintains good condition. He will need to be fed plenty of fresh, raw meat and ample protein and so on if he is going to keep in good bloom. Never expect too much sense at mating time from a dog who has been celibate for three years. Often a dog of this category has no idea what to do when he is introduced to a bitch in full heat. If they are worth using, such dogs may need a good deal of reassurance and perhaps manipulative assistance in order to effect a proper mating.

Pre—natal Care

German Shepherd Dogs do not always easily reveal to the eye that they are in whelp until quite near the end of the normal term of gestation, which is sixty—three days. However, it is very important to start preparing for the hoped—for litter. The bitch's prime condition must be her owner's first thought. She must be exercised quite normally every day and groomed in the usual way but should be guided well away from any activity which might be harmful such as fighting, falling into the river, and so on. Admittedly, she might well do all these things were she in the wild state, but she is a domestic creature these days and has softened to suit, as one might say. She may need to be wormed; this should be discussed with your veterinary surgeon, although there are many reliable remedies on the market these days. The vet will advise also about injections. The modern bitch is beset with a number of infections which fall mainly into the streptococcal and staphylococcal categories. Your professional man will know what to do to avoid fading puppies (whelps which eventually die after a miserable week's life) and absorption (when no puppies arrive after what appears a normal pregnancy).

German Shepherd Dog litters are quite big, sometimes as many as a dozen, although from five to ten is quite normal: six is ideal. This means that not only the dam but also the whelps she is carrying need to be built up. This can be achieved not only with good and perhaps improved feeding but also with extra nourishment, including calcium phosphate sources: milk is especially important.

Prepare a whelping box or suitable place for your bitch. If you use a box (such as is shown in the sketch), make certain that it is very big and roomy. If she has the maximum number of puppies, space will be needed. The box should allow room for the dam to lie down in comfort with her puppies. The 'pig-rail' will give a small puppy some protection from the danger of being squashed by a

Adamant of Viewdowns
at 14 months
owned by Mr L.Bush

Ch.Novem Bolero
owned by
Messrs Dunkley, Woods
and Wilmot.
(Photo: Diane Pearce)

clumsy mother; the front can be let down for easy access and exit if required. A piece of laundered and disinfected hessian is ideal for affixing to the bottom of the box, but it is as well to let the bitch do the actual whelping either on the bare board of the base or on newspapers; these can be gathered up and disposed of at will and replaced by fresh papers immediately. The bitch should be introduced to her new quarters about ten days before she is due to whelp. Do not expect her to react kindly to them if you delay until a few hours before her litter arrives. She will have enough to think about at this time without the distraction of a strange bed. Never use straw or blankets in the whelping box; the puppies may crawl out of sight underneath them and could be in danger of being squashed if the bitch cannot readily see them.

Make sure that you have informed your veterinary surgeon of the expected date of whelping. You might need him in an emergency, and you will know that he is available should an urgent call be necessary.

NB Take in whelping box pic

The Whelping

As the time when she will have her puppies draws closer you will observe that the bitch becomes steadily less relaxed: just before the actual whelping she will show every sign of restlessness, even agitation. This will involve some turning around on herself, sudden braking when moving, and clear indication of worry: all this is more evident in a maiden bitch than in one who has experienced it all before. These symptoms are often evident for two or three days prior to the actual day of whelping, by which time her temperature, which is normally 101.4 degrees Fahrenheit will have dropped to 100 degrees or 97.5 degrees, when she is about to deliver her young. A cautious breeder will find this a good and safe guide that labour is about to commence.

The bitch will probably refuse all meals just prior to whelping and will fall into a deep sleep; this will set her up well for the coming ardours of whelping. When you see her in this state, arrange that she is left well alone and not in any way distracted by strangers or other dogs, even those well known to her. The room temperature should be not less than 70 degrees F.

When the bitch awakens, she will probably be ready to start whelping; she will intimate this by scratching at the floor of her box and show signs of general restlessness. You should have ready by you in the whelping room a number of first—aid items, including:

(a) paper tissues
(b) surgical lint cut into 10 inch (254mm) squares or any other convenient size
(c) sharp, probe-pointed surgical scissors, sterilized
(d) surgical cotton, cut into pieces about 6 inches (152mm) long
(e) an antiseptic disinfectant
(f) petroleum jelly in tube or jar
(g) a supply of cotton wool
(h) odd pieces of clean washed towelling or face flannels
(i) hot water bottle (the old fashioned stone variety is best) covered with cloth or a sock for protection
(j) feeding bottle or pipette
(k) kettle of water, ready plugged in to the mains or on the gas, plus a box of matches
(l) brandy, small teaspoon. This is for the bitch, for her puppies (in which case

absolute minimal measures should be given), or for yourself !

(m)   general food and sustenance for yourself

(n)   plenty of old newspapers

(o)   basin or bowl

Obviously, you can make your own selection from these requisites, but the purpose of the exercise is to be ready with the the things you might need rather than have to search around for them at a time when your presence may well be better employed alongside your bitch while she is whelping.

The bitch will soon commence to strain, the periods of labour becoming more frequent as she gets near to delivering her first puppy. If you think it prudent, offer her a little warm milk. She may or may not accept it, but it often has the effect of hastening the arrival of her first–born. However, it is usually better to leave her well alone — do not feed her, do not talk to her, just let her get on with the task. If everything proceeds normally, a small water–filled bag will appear at the mouth of the vulva. This is a sort of cushion or buffer which will protect the oncoming puppy when it greets the outside world. The bitch's muscular contractions will eventually rend the bag, the puppy soon following in a membraneous sac, head first. By licking vigorously, the bitch will break the sac, releasing the puppy together with a great deal of fluid, which will be soaked up by the newspapers lining the whelping box. After its buffeting by the bitch's tongue the puppy will soon commence to breathe, even to squeak with apparent peevishness. It will be attached by its umbilical cord to the afterbirth (placenta), and the bitch will instinctively sever the cord close to the whelp's navel with a sharp nip. If she seems unable or disinclined to conduct this operation it must be done for her. Take one of the ready–prepared lengths of surgical thread and tie it tightly round the cord about 1 inch (25cm) up the umbilical cord from the puppy's navel. Then cut the cord with the sterilized scissors about 1 inch (25mm) above the tie you have made. Sometimes the bitch will devour the afterbirth; if this happens, so well and good it will do her no harm as it is a perfectly natural action. If she does not eat it, then dispose of it for her. Sometimes the afterbirth remains in the womb: in this case it has to be withdrawn gently or it will decompose and cause what will probably amount to an asceptic condition. Do this by drawing carefully and directly on the hanging cord until it is quite free from the bitch's body.

The first puppy sometimes takes a long while to appear, although German Shepherd puppies generally breed easily as they are reasonably 'streamlined' in head and body. If a puppy is stubborn in coming through or if its position seems abnormal, then it may need assistance. Breech births — when the feet or rear

62

end is presented first are easy enough to deal with. The visible part is gripped gently with one of the towel pieces you have ready and the puppy is withdrawn without ado. If you have to do this make sure that you do it with all speed if the bag is already broken, but take care that you do not squeeze the whelp's body in your anxiety. Try to effect the withdrawal in rhythm with the natural straining of the dam: effective speed is of great importance. If you feel doubtful about your ability to perform such a task, then it is better to call in your veterinary surgeon. He will also be able to deal with any retained placentae with an injection of *Pitruitrin*.

The bitch will usually sleep or doze between deliveries, and this should be encouraged as she is gathering her energies in this way. Usually, if she has managed to deliver three without trouble the rest will follow automatically, the intervals between puppies often varying quite considerably. As she progresses you should try to find opportunities to clear up. Large dogs such as the German Shepherd make quite a lot of mess when whelping, especially with the bulk of water which is released at every birth. Once the bitch seems to have finished, try to persuade her to go outside and relieve herself and give her a bowl of warm milk to encourage her. Once she is outside you can start a quick tidy – up, putting the puppies into a basket nearby and disposing of the soiled newspapers at once. Check every puppy for its sex, and make sure that no abnormalities exist. Provided that you are satisfied that there are no more puppies to come, you can leave the bitch to her own devices for a while and this will give you a chance to compose yourself. If you have any lingering doubts then you should seek the opinion of your veterinary surgeon, although once a bitch has settled down and the puppies are sucking away merrily at her there is very little chance of further births and all should be well.

The most useful size of litter is from five to seven. Although German Shepherd bitch's are able to cope with more, she will make the best of six, which is really enough for any dam. If you have a larger litter than this, you may consider culling or using a foster mother. Foster mothers are often advertised in the canine press. Certain kennels specialize in supplying good clean bitches (often Collies) for the purpose. With a litter say of nine German Shepherds you can put five on to the natural dam, four on to the Collie, and this way you should get maximum results. For the first four days it is best to keep the entire litter on the German Shepherd, for then they will *all* get the benefit of her initial milk flow, which contains Colostrum; which is not only a mild laxative but is also highly nourishing, being of prime value to them. Make sure that every puppy is given a fair share of the feeding. The inguinal teats are most plenteous in their supply. These are the large teats in the lower regions, and you should ensure that each puppy is placed there in his turn and watched so that he is not pushed off by greedier members of the litter. In the initial stages, the bitch can be fed with a sustaining drink of warm milk to which a teaspoonful of glucose or a dessert spoonful of honey has been added. She should have plenty of milk to drink as this will aid and build up her own milk supply.

Post Whelping Problems

Eclampsia
Eclampsia is a common occurrence after whelping, although it can happen shortly before a bitch delivers her puppies. It is a sort of milk fever and brings on restlessness and nervousness, accompanied by panting. The condition is caused by a deficiency of calcium and vitamin **D**. It can be rectified by injections of calcium in the form of *Collo Cal D* preparation. Keep an eye on dam and puppies every hour after whelping. Eclampsia can occur even three or four weeks after the puppies' arrival, and the danger period is not over until after weaning has been completed.

Aglactia
Aglactia is lack of milk; a condition quite common in modern bitches. The dam suddenly acquires a high temperature which prevents her milk passing through the teats to her puppies. She often panics, and the puppies state their displeasure quite audibly. As a rule the condition persists for two to three days, which is rather worrying as a milk flow in the initial stages is important. Loss of Colostrum to the puppies is a cause for concern.

A bitch will often improve after just a few hours of suffering this distressing condition, and she can be helped by continually pressing the puppies to her teats. If this proves of no avail, call in the veterinary surgeon. He will inject the bitch, thereby reducing her temperature, and once normal body heat has returned the milk will flow normally and the puppies feed and thrive happily.

Metritis
Metritis is a condition which may result from the retention of the last born puppy's placenta in the dam's womb, although it can be caused by even small particles of membrane which have been left behind. There is often an unpleasant septic discharge from the vulva, and the bitch will be in considerable discomfort,

the milk flow being disrupted and the puppies clearly indisposed. Inflammation of the uterus is normally noted about a week after the whelping, and the bitch's temperature and pulse rate will be high. The condition must be attended to urgently, and the veterinary surgeon may well have to act immediately in order to save her. Naturally, a bitch in this state will be unable to care for her puppies properly, and the entire litter will have to be removed and either put on a foster dam or hand−reared.

Hand−rearing

This is by no means an easy task. It requires immense patience, and the person doing it needs to be dedicated to the task. The entire litter has to be fed as one, i.e. no individual puppy (unless he is a weakling) can be treated differently from his brother or sister. The weakling may need extra attention, although frankly, if the litter to be hand−reared is only a day or so old and contains a weakling then it is better and kinder to have it painlessly destroyed. 'Lactol' is a good substitute for bitch's milk, although there is no true substitute for the real thing. Instructions for mixing and for hand−rearing will be found on the container, and great care should be taken to ensure that these are closely followed. It is very important to keep to precise quantities of food and exact times of feeding. The temperature of the food is also vitally important, and fresh food is necessary at every meal. There are a number of ways of administering the food to a small puppy, but care must be taken neither to over−feed nor to feed too fast. Keep the cup of 'Lactol' mixture in a bowl of warm water so that the temperature of the food can be maintained; this will ensure that, when the last puppy in the litter comes to be fed, his food will be at the same correct temperature as that of the first member. The attitude of the puppies is a good guide as to whether they are being fed properly and are content. Happy puppies will settle down to sleep after they have been fed and cleaned up; unsettled youngsters will cry incessantly and pass motions which instead of being of firm porridge−like consistency and brown in colour are loose and yellow. Such indications are sufficient to warn the hand−rearer that the mixture he is feeding the puppies is too strong and needs to be diluted. The youngsters should be weighed daily and exact records kept, and each puppy must be examined closely to ensure that its condition is getting progressively better.

Once a puppy has been fed, wipe his face, especially his nose and lips, with a swab of damp cotton wool. This will remove milk which has settled there after his feed and prevent any waste from congealing. If she were present, the dam would keep her puppies clean and lick and buffet them around their genitals and rear parts to induce urination and the passing of motions. This action must therefore be simulated artificially, by soaking a wad of cotton wool in warm water and stroking their genitals gently with it. Once the motions have been passed, smear a little petroleum jelly around the genitals and anus. No puppy should be allowed to remain constipated. In one so young this can prove fatal. If any youngster fails to pass his main motion after his meal, grease a veterinary thermometer and insert it fractionally into the rectum. This will invariably stimulate the required motion.

It is a good idea to install an infra—red lamp when you are maintaining an orphan litter deprived of its dam's body warmth. These lamps are available from the better pet stores and are advertised in the canine weeklies. The lamp should be suspended from the ceiling and set to produce a constant temperature of between 75 and 80 degrees Fahrenheit (24 and 26.5 Centigrade) at least for the first three days. After this the heat can be reduced to maintain 60 degrees Fahrenheit (15.5 Centigrade) but this should be done gradually, by reducing the lamp a little each day. A dull—emitter bulb should be used, as this is considered harmless to the youngsters' eyes when they open about ten days after birth. Place a wire guard around the lamp reflector to provide added security, in case the bulb should break loose and fall to the ground.

In spite of all the time you will spend in hand—rearing and the sleep that you cannot fail to lose in the process, you will experience a great and lasting satisfaction when the job is complete, and you will realize how wonderfully fit and well the litter of German Shepherds that you *might* have lost looks.

Dew—claws

The dew—claw is the rudimentary fifth digit which is equivalent to the thumb in a human. It appears on the insides of the puppy's forelegs, just above the feet. Sometimes dew—claws will be noted on the hind limbs too, and these are particularly objectionable. Remove the dew-claws when the puppy is about four days old; if they are left they can prove a nuisance in later life by getting entangled and becoming torn, quite apart from the fact that they can spoil a dog's gait. The operation can be done by the competent breeder, although most people prefer a veterinary surgeon to do it. If you decide to tackle it, use a pair of sharp, snub—nosed surgical scissors; making a swift cut, then brush in or dab on with cotton wool some permanganate of potash to stem the bleeding. The wounds should be examined at least once a day until they have healed.

Chapter 4

Feeding

Weaning and Puppy Feeding

How well you wean your puppies will affect their future health and appearance. The dam will normally take responsibility for their milk up to say the age of one month, but if she has had a big litter to care for she is likely to need some assistance by the time her family is three weeks old. This assumes that the bitch's milk has been adequate in volume and of good quality. It will soon become apparent from her puppies' coats and condition if either of these factors is at fault; if so, you will then have to start weaning very early. Bitch's milk is essential to the brood while they can get it , and no other milk compares with it — as far as the puppies are concerned, of course. In *The Complete Dog Breeder's Manual* (1954), Clifford Hubbard gives an interesting table which reveals the difference between the milk of a bitch and that of four other familiar animals.

Analyses of Milk

Animal	Sugar	Casein, etc.	Fat	Salts	Water
Dog	3·1	8·0	12·0	1·2	75·5
Goat	4·75	4·0	6·25	1·0	84·0
Cat	5·2	7·9	3·65	0·9	82·35
Cow	4·85	3·75	3·7	0·6	87·1
Sheep	4·95	4·7	5·2	0·7	84·45

'Lactol' is excellent for weaning and can be prepared as a substitute for bitch's milk. Instructions will be found with the preparation; carefully refer to what is written about the age of youngsters. The milk is normally fed at blood heat and, as in hand–rearing, the mixture should be stood in a cup which in turn stands in a bowl of hot water . This will ensure that the first and last puppy in the litter are fed milk at the same heat. It is not difficult to get a small puppy to lap; just smear a little of the preparation under his lips and wait for it to be taken in. At first, progress will be slow, but once the youngster gets the taste he will start to lap with enthusiasm. Every puppy has to be fed individually at first; once you have them all lapping with confidence they can be introduced to a communal feeding dish. By this time the dam's personal burden of feeding will have been eased a little, and although her puppies will still be at her teats at least they will not be dragging at her excessively. Before putting down the feeding bowl, make sure that they have not been near the dam for an hour or more previously. They will then approach their prepared meal with good appetites.

German Shepherd puppies are not gluttons like some breed's youngsters, but exceptions do occur. The average puppy can be left to get on with his meal without being hogged by his fellows, but the exceptions may need to be controlled, so watch them all the time when they are eating. Try to keep the feeding trough a little off the ground. This will ensure that the puppies will not fall into the food and it will aid towards a better head posture and improve the youngster's general bearing.

Feeding can be stepped up from the 'Lactol' routine after three or four days. The extra diet can include minced boiled tripe, poached egg, and light milk puddings, also finely shredded or minced raw fresh meat. The meat should be introduced in easy stages and the quantity should be increased gradually until it represents about fifty percent of the intake. Care should be taken to avoid putting too much food down at one time. To avoid distension and digestive discomforts, it is best to divide a normal daily intake into four or five 'sittings' spread over a twelve hour period. By the time the puppies are six weeks old they will have become quite big; at this age they will be increasing weight by 3 lb.(1.3kg) a week. At about this time, maybe even earlier, the dam herself will be disgorging some of her food for the puppies benefit. This is a natural action and need not perturb a breeder who has not witnessed it before, though its advantages are mixed. The puppies will rush at the partly−digested food and gobble it up, so you should make sure that the meals which you give to the dam do not contain food which is too rich for puppies or is too large for their gullets. Also, if the dam is allowed to disgorge food too often she will fall badly out of condition, which should not be allowed to happen at this time. In fact, she must now be well built up with high-protein food with plenty of raw fresh meat, although fluids can be cut down severely as her milk supply must be minimal.

The puppies themselves should be drinking plenty of milk, as milk is essential for their good growth and bone. At six weeks of age they will be on four meals a day, comprising two meat meals and two milky feeds, given to them alternately. By now they should be quite independent of their dam's milk supply, even of her presence. The amount of food will need to be increased for the amount and quality will determine their rate of development in the next few months. Do not over-stuff them; it is important to keep an eye on them as they feed, as you will soon gain an intimate knowledge of each puppy's requirements and learn a lot about his eating idiosyncrasies in this way. In the seventh week you can reduce the actual number of meals to three. This does not mean that the quantity must be reduced, quite the opposite in fact, because as a puppy grows he needs more food.

During the whole of the puppy—rearing term from weaning to complete independence it is important to inspect every youngster after his meal. The nose and mouth will need wiping over to obviate encrustment of waste food, and the under tail area and the genitals should be examined after motions have been passed and cleaned up if necessary.

Worming

The worm commonly encountered in puppies is the Roundworm. This is a parasite, looking like vermicelli, and creamy-white in colour, and all puppies are thought to be infested to a greater or lesser degree. The dam herself probably passes them on to her embryonic young, but they are acquired easily enough by puppies from the faeces of infected dogs, or from eggs which are taken orally from their dam's teats in the course of feeding.

The infested puppy seldom thrives until the pest has been eradicated. His appetite usually falls off, although instances have been noted where an appetite has become ravenous. The coat inclines to 'stare' and divide, while motions seem 'jellied' or very loose, indicating an upset stomach. There are many good proprietary vermifuges and vermicides on the market today, and the average owner prefers to use one of these quite early in the youngster's life. At one time it was not considered prudent to worm a puppy before it was at least five weeks but veterinary medicine now permits earlier dosing and there are no ill-effects. For those who do not fancy the task of worming their puppies, the veterinary surgeon will attend to the matter for a nominal fee. When expelled (if a vermifuge is used) the worms will appear in a tightly knit skein and will probably surprise you by their number. Burn them at once and disinfect the area of operations, at the same time cleaning up the relieved puppy in his anal region.

The tapeworm is rather different. It attaches itself by a sort of hook to the intestinal wall and is made up of a number of segments which are small at the head end but gradually increase in size towards the 'tail' or opposite end. Each segment is really a worm in its own right and on breaking away from the main stem and being passed through its host becomes ingested by an animal such as the sheep, horse, rabbit, or fox. A flea can pass the worm on to the dog, who can also acquire the parasite from the viscera of an infected 'produce' animal or 'caught' rabbit.

This worm is less frequently met than the Roundworm, but its effect is rather less pleasant. As a rule you will notice it when the grain—like segments which comprise the main shaft of the worm adhere to the dog's anus or are evident in his motions. It is best to ask your veterinary surgeon to deal with this worm, as he is more likely to do so effectively (it is quite often several feet long !) than you would with a home remedy. Once the worm has been expelled, the dog's condition will improve noticeably within a few days, his coat will become glossy and healthy, and the strong body odours, so evident in dogs with Tapeworm will disappear.

Note that before being sold every puppy should be wormed (for Roundworm) this should be done at least three days before he goes. The breeder should make sure that the worming has not adversely affected the youngster's stomach and that his motions are firm and healthy by the time he leaves for his new home and owner.

Adult Feeding

What the dog would eat were he in the wild state may be a useful guide to feeding, but it should not be followed slavishly. The dog today is domesticated and his modified chemical make-up to a large extent governs his particular requirements.

However, it is important that his staple diet is fresh raw meat. By all means get him accustomed to eating lightly—cooked meat, canned proprietary dog foods, carefully boned steamed white fish, and so on. But do so conscious of the fact that your motives are selfish ones: because it will be more convenient to you as his owner to feed him with this provender (however excellent it may be) if you cannot lay your hands on the fresh raw meat. Too many dogs today, having been fed solely on meat, will refuse all other kinds of food, and such a dog can prove to be a worry to his owner at times.

A dog prefers his meat in large lumps so that he can tear off the pieces he wants to eat and enjoy it at will. Few dog—owners feed their dogs in this way, preferring instead to cut up the meat into manageable chunks which they know the dog will eat easily without risk of choking. The meat used should be butcher's meat: shin of beef being particularly beneficial, although not always at a price to suit all pockets. Many breeders complain at the cost of butcher's meat, which is certainly high, and it seems sensible if you cannot afford to keep a dog on such food to try and adapt him to meals which will cost less and probably will provide for his needs equally well! There are so many prepared dog foods on the market today, most of them offered by highly reputable firms with up-to-date laboratories and factories, that one cannot lightly reject them when planning a dog's menu at an economic price. Some people think highly of ox cheek, offal, paunches, and such things. These are good, but like liver, they give best results when fed once a week only. Dog biscuits are essential: there are many different varieties to choose from, and you will soon get to know what your dog likes best and what suits him. Following any trial of biscuits or a new type of food, always keep an eye on the dog's main motion that day and on the following two days. This will tell you if the food suits his stomach or not.

Erracht's Britta
owned by Mrs J.A.Cameron   (Photo: Diane Pearce)

Fish is excellent food for the dog, and your fishmonger will have quite a large variety of suitable cheap fish, but again fish should be on the menu not more than twice a week at the most. Fish should be used, like some of the canned foods, more as a variation to the diet or to add zest to an ordinary dish rather than as a staple food. Always make sure that every bone has been removed. It is better fed either boiled or steamed; the dog will gain more nutrients in this way. Eggs and milk are, of course, essentials, especially milk, and a dog ought to have a bowl of fresh milk daily. Vegetables and potatoes are not suitable for dogs and if forced upon them usually cause digestive upsets. The dog himself knows this instinctively and confines himself as a rule to green grass which he eats, often as an emetic.

Considering his size, the German Shepherd dog is not a huge eater and can exist on a single meal a day, say 2 lb. (0.907kg.) of meat, an amount usually sufficient for breeds half his size. The breeder must always strive to maintain a certain standard of condition and muscle. Obviously, if your dog looks scrawny and thin it is reasonable to assume that he is not getting enough meat, and the amount must be increased accordingly. If a German Shepherd appears hungry then he can be fed more, for the breed is not a greedy one, unlike the Pug which will go on eating almost to bursting point! Always keep an eye on your dog when he is feeding. You will see how he tackles his meal; if a German Shepherd goes through it quickly and seems to seek more then he probably wants more. If he gets two—thirds of the way through the meal and then becomes disinterested, eating the rest as though he could not care less, then you are probably putting down a little too much.

All dog-feeding and husbandry is largely a matter of common sense. You should get to know your dog so well that you become aware of any variation, however slight, which arises in his manner or make—up. Additives, such as 'Vetzymes'(a Phillips Yeast Product), are extremely useful, creating a healthy appetite in the dog and aiding his mental outlook quite noticeably. Most breeders keep a stock of these useful tablets and have found them extremely beneficial. Cod—liver oil is useful in the winter months, and olive oil is best used when the weather is hot. Malt extract is recommended as a body—builder. It is not necessary to give more than one teaspoonful of these oils daily to any adult dog. Cod—liver oil is conveniently available in veterinary form. Vitamins can also be obtained in capsules and in tablets, and these can be used with advantage, although it is advisable to have the doses prescribed by your veterinary surgeon, or other professional adviser. 'Abidec' can be bought in liquid or capsule form and is good for administering vitamins **A,B,C,D,**and **E**. 'Calsimil' and 'Collo Cal **D**', which contain a balanced form of calcium for dogs with phosphorus and vitamin **D**, are two preparations particularly good for curbing excitability in a nursing dam or to replace calcium deficiency.

Never feed poultry or game unless you give only the carved flesh. The bones are very dangerous to a dog and although your German Shepherd may catch a rabbit and eat it the same day without harm, if the carcass is left to be eaten the next day, the hardened bones will constitute a real danger to him.

CHAPTER 5

General Management

Training

No one enjoys having an ill−trained dog, and it is clear at times that the dog himself does not enjoy being ill−trained! He does not want to be continually reprimanded and shouted at, which is what so many owners have to do merely because they have not bothered to show their dog what to do and how to do it. A badly−trained dog reflects on the owner's lack of ability at training and becomes a possession which is not appreciated as a good dog should be. The real German Shepherd has a strong and positive character with a natural ability to obey; he is also a big, powerful dog. Firm handling is therefore essential in order to maintain him comfortably in the family circle and to train him to do what you want rather than have him do what he wants.

Most people prefer to train a puppy. It is simpler, for you are starting with virgin material, as no one else has had a hand in shaping or mis−shaping the animal's behaviour. But be firm right from the beginning; too many owners laugh and enjoy a young puppy's early capers, its exuberance and clumsiness, only to realize too late that the dog has grown up and acquired some irritating ways as normal habits! It then becomes rather difficult to break him of these unwanted characteristics, and it certainly isn't possible without a good deal of pressure on the part of the trainer.

In the Home

The first lesson a puppy must learn is house-cleanliness. German Shepherd Dogs make quite large puddles, and the sooner a youngster is encouraged to perform his natural functions outside the better. If he lives in a flat, a sand–tray will have to be used; in a house he must learn to use the garden. The first word he must learn to understand is 'no'. Thus when he makes a puddle he should be picked up, taken to it, and shown it quite closely. At the same time say 'no' quite forcefully so that he knows you are annoyed. Then either set him firmly on to the sand-tray, holding him there for a few moments, or put him outside in the garden and close the door on him. He will soon catch on. His training can be helped if you remember that a small puppy sleeps a great deal and that when he wakes up he will invariably want to urinate. Keep an eye on him while he is asleep, and the instant he wakes up pick him up without waiting for him to amble around and set him at once either on his sand-tray or outside in the garden. Keep him there and watch until he has passed his motion. If you do this every

Tramella Flame
owned by Mr J.A. & Mrs C.E.Barker   (Photo: Diane Pearce)

time, before long you will have him properly trained, going straight to the tray or the door as soon as he wakes up. Remember though, that if by chance you are not there to open the door or to see him on to his tray he must not be blamed: it is your fault for not being around to help him. Make sure that you never scold him in such circumstances, and remember to praise him when he does correctly what he has been trained to do. At night, he is sure to forget himself and who can blame a puppy for making a puddle during a lonely six or eight – hour period If you keep him in the kitchen at night, cover the floor with old newspapers, so that in the morning you can quickly gather these up and dispose of them together with the mess that he has made.

Never leave an untrained puppy in a room where he can create damage. People will tell you at times that their new puppy has torn up furniture, cushions, slippers, and such things. It is not the puppy's fault — it is theirs for leaving a raw youngster in a place where it could do such damage. Make sure that small puppies are either left in completely bare rooms or are boxed when you go out or retire for the night. Never chastise a puppy or he will lose faith and confidence in you, and the retention of these loyalties is very important if you are to train him successfully. Some trainers like to have a rolled – up newspaper to emphasize the word 'no' during their training. The newspaper makes a lot of noise but it does not hurt. It is often effective to synchronize its use with the word of command. Later, as the puppy become better educated, it can be dispensed with, the word 'no' alone will be sufficient to get good results.

On the Lead
The young German Shepherd will need to learn all about the outside world as soon as possible. Up to the age of four months, by when he will have had all his protective innoculations, he can be trained on the leash within your garden or home. Put him on a slip lead and lead him up and down the garden; always keep him on your left – hand side so that he learns a straight and steady action without pulling or dragging back. Keep such training to no more than ten minutes at a time so that the dog does not get bored or stale at the work. Keep the rolled up newspaper by you during this period. If the pupil pulls forward on the leash, thereby throwing out his shoulders, tap him on the muzzle with the newspaper and give the command 'back' or 'heel'. He will soon learn that he must not pull forward. If he draws behind, dragging his rear along the ground, he must be enouraged to come forward with words of reassurance or by bribing him with a titbit, together with a firm pull on the leash which will jerk him into forward action.

Once the pupil has shown promise he can be taken into the outside world. At first, he may be bemused at the noise and bustle, but this will soon pass off, and he will move forward with confidence. Later, when he is ready for show training, you will already have instilled the elementary lessons into him.

Children

German Shepherds are very protective and highly sensitive. They seem to like children and make good members of a family circle where children live and play. As with all breeds it is best to have the children first and the dog afterwards, introducing the dog as a small puppy so that he enters the family and grows up in it. Then he will take over almost as a nursemaid to the younger members of the home.

Exercise

The breed can take a great deal of exercise, but it must not be overdone. If you keep a number of dogs and puppies, it is wise to allow a generous run outside every kennel. Then dogs will exercise at will, and the puppies will usually play until they are ready to sleep. The wise owner never leaves any item, toy, or food around in the kennel over which a quarrel could arise. Regular walking exercise on the lead is a good thing for the German Shepherd. Let him loose in the wide-open spaces but make sure that no small pet dog is running free. German Shepherds are herding dogs, and it is their nature to 'round up' any living moving object. The average German Shepherd can keep up for miles with a horseman out for a canter and can easily cover many miles on foot; he can quite outdistance his owner. The author recommends quiet country roads for this practice. A dog will cover ten miles or so at a brisk trot without in the least slackening his enthusiasm. This is the ideal exercise for the dog's feet and it is a healthful way of exercising the breed.

Care should be taken in exercising young puppies. Overdoing the daily routine can ruin a youngster and even with a dog such as the German Shepherd his exercise time should be increased gradually as the dog grows. It is best to train your dog to walk on a slack lead: cinder and rough paths are better than grass for his feet. Regularity is the key—note for success in exercising, which is a dog's most important need after his food. If the weather is inclement never let him down by staying indoors and depriving him of his outing.

Ch.Nyta of Duconer
owned by
Miss D.Mitchell
(Photo: Diane Pearce)

Ch.Vonjen Nijinsky,
owned by
Mrs A.Jenkins
(Photo: Diane Pearce)

Grooming

To look at a German Shepherd you would think that his coat must present an owner with many problems of care and attention. Oddly enough, this is not so, and the breed seems to have a unique coat, as it is very shiny and not inclined to carry dirt or dust. Of course, it should receive daily attention in the form of brushing and combing, but it is not necessary to wash it as regularly as is required in some breeds. This is indeed fortunate, for bathing a German Shepherd Dog is quite a task and can seldom be done by one person. If it does become necessary you should start at the tail first, washing part of the coat and body while working towards the head. A thorough drying–down with warm towels in an even temperature should then follow; and when the dog is dry take him out for a brisk canter to get the blood circulating well. Trimming is not needed with this breed, though plenty of attention with the brush and comb usually pays handsome dividends. The ideal brush has well–spaced bristles set in a rubber pad base. These are available at any good pet store. At grooming time check the dog's eyes, ears, teeth, and gums, and under and round the tail, making sure that these areas are healthy and clean. The breed's moulting tendencies are well known; dogs shed their coats rather less than bitches, but plenty of other breeds moult more profusely, and in the German Shepherd moulting lasts for only a short time.

Guarding

The German Shepherd can be trained to be an aggressive guard. This is useful in industry in view of its size and power. However, an owner will find that his dog will have a strong deterrent effect on would–be intruders. Once upset, the breed can prove very formidable, and since it is quite possessive of territory a dog can easily be trained to guard both home and owner. Note, however, that the breed is not particularly vociferous.

Kennel or Indoors ?

There seems no point in providing a kennel for a German Shepherd Dog kept as a pet. He should be part of the family circle and live indoors with his own bed, and trained to conform to the usual rules and regulations of the home. Most families can find a space for a pet even as large as the German Shepherd. If they cannot, then in fairness to the dog they should never have bought one ! There are some strong and useful canvas − based beds for dogs on the market, although it is not always easy to procure the really large ones of the kind that you will require. A German Shepherd's bed should be 36 by 30 inches (914 x 762mm) rather bigger if you can manage it. It should be raised about 5 or 6 inches (127 − 152mm) off the floor for comfort and to avoid under − door draughts.

Given such accommodation for his sleeping hours the dog is well set up. He will quickly learn what is wanted of him and know when to be 'seen and not heard'. His intelligence and mental reflexes will be developed better than if he were kept alone in an outdoor kennel; not only will he enjoy life more but he will give you, as his owner, much additional pleasure too.

Of course, if you keep a number of dogs of this breed you must kennel them. There are a number of good pre − fabricated kennels available — models to suit all breeds and most pockets. If you buy one, or make one to your own specifications, make sure that it is large enough for the dogs to move around comfortably. Every kennel should have its own run, which should be strongly constructed and with walls of sufficient height, as German Shepherds are great jumpers. The great advantage of the run system is that the dog can get plenty of fresh air, can play freely with others, and can attend to his functions outside instead of inside the kennel. Make the kennel high enough for yourself and visitors to stand inside without crouching, you should allow at least 6 feet (1.8 metres) from floor to ceiling if this is practicable. Assuming that you intend to start a kennel which is to become established as a breeding and exhibiting venture, you will need four connecting kennels, as well as a single one placed well away from them to be used as a 'hospital' bed if needed. Try to arrange for a small cupboard to be built on to the end of the main range of four in which you can keep all the paraphernalia of the kennel − brooms, brushes, pails, shovels, wood wool, sawdust and disinfectant. Four kennels will keep any novice busy for a time; then, when you are ready to graduate to something more ambitious, you can add to the range, providing space permits.

Try to arrange for the kennels to be built on well drained gravel or sandy soil, preferably facing south or south − west. If you can arrange it, position them so that existing trees protect them from prevailing winds, but do not position them under trees. The whole structure should be raised well off the ground, and the kennel floors should be of wood. If any refinements are to be introduced, then include slide − out sleeping benches as these can be removed and scrubbed easily. Whereas with the German Shepherd you do not have to worry about heating in the winter months — he does not seem to need it — ventilation and complete freedom from draughts are essential. The runs themselves should be laid of well pressed—down cinder or screened breeze to a depth of at least 6 inches (152 mm). This will allow for good drainage and is better than concrete not only for this reason but also because it keeps the dog's feet trim and well knit. The best form of bedding is wood—wool, and although the dogs seem to like straw better it is inclined to harbour vermin and one cannot always guarantee its perfect cleanliness.

Try to install electric light in the kennel but ensure that all cables and connections enter the kennel at points where they are inaccessible to the dogs, although German Shepherds are no worse when it comes to chewing things than other breeds. Scrupulous hygiene must be observed at all times: go into every nook and cranny with disinfectant and scrub down the exterior with a strong antiseptic germicide.

Obedience and Security Training

Obedience and security training, is of course, a very different matter to the elementary form already discussed, which is really no more than a series of exercises calculated to keep a dog manageable around the house for his own happiness and that of his owner.

Obedience and security training in its professional form is highly skilled work. Depending on the form it takes and the job for which it is intended, training is based on a close study and understanding of a dog's mind and his abilities.

Specialized books and advanced training classes are readily available to the owner whose interests extend to these matters. It is not within the compass of this volume to include material that really requires a whole book to itself. But for those readers who are interested in this advanced form of training, I reproduce here the Kennel Club Regulations for Tests for Obedience Classes, Working Trials, and the various Stakes together with some selected explanatory notes.

Kennel Club Regulations for Tests for Obedience Classes S(2) 1st May 1976
Beginners — If owner or handler or dog have won a total of two or more first prizes in the Beginners Class, they may not compete in Beginners. Winners of one first prize in any other

80

Obedience Class are ineligible to compete in this Class. Handlers will not be penalized for encouragement or extra commands except in the Sit and Down tests. In these tests, at the discretion of the judge, handlers may face their dogs. Judges or stewards must not use the words 'last command' except in the Sit and Down tests.

1. Heel on Lead. (15 points)
2. Heel Free. (20 points)
3. Recall from sit or down position at handler's choice. Dog to be recalled by the handler when stationary and facing the dog. Dog to return smartly to handler, sit in front, go to heel — all on command of judge or steward to handler. Distance at discretion of judge. Test commences when handler leaves dog.(10 points)
4. Retrieve any article. Handlers may use their own article. (25 points)
5. Sit one minute, handler in sight. (10 points)
6. Down two minutes, handler in sight. (20 points)

Total 100 points

Novice — For dogs that have not won two first prizes in Obedience Classes (Beginners Class excepted). Handlers will not be penalized for encouragement or extra commands except in the Sit and Down tests. In these tests, at the discretion of the judge, handlers may face their dogs. Judges or stewards must not use the words 'last command' except in the sit and down tests.

1. Temperament Test. To take place immediately before heel on lead. Dog to be on lead in the Stand position. Handler to stand by dog. Judge to approach quietly from the front and to run his hand gently down the dog's back. Judge may talk quietly to the dog to reassure it. Any undue resentment, cringing, growling or snapping to be penalized. This is not a stand for examination or stay test. (10 points)
2. Heel on Lead (10 points)
3. Heel Free (20 points)
4. Recall from sit or down position at handler's choice. Dog to be recalled by handler when stationary and facing the dog. Dog to return smartly to handler, sit in front, go to heel — all on command of judge or steward to handler. Distance at discretion of the judge. Test commences when handler leaves dog. (10 points)
5. Retrieve a dumb−bell. Handlers may use their own bells. (20 points)
6. Sit one minute, handler in sight. (10 points)
7. Down two minutes, handler in sight. (20 points)

Total 100 points

Class A — For dogs which have not won four first prizes in Classes A and B in total. Simultaneous command and signal will be permitted. Extra commands or signals must be penalized.

1. Heel on Lead. (15 points)
2. Temperament Test. Will take place before Heel Free. Dog to be in the stand position and off lead. Handler to stand beside dog. Conditions as for Novice Temperament Test, except that Test will commence with order 'last command' and end with order 'test finished'. Extra commands to be penalized. This is not a stand for examination or stay test. (10 points)
3. Heel Free. (20 points)
4. Recall from Sit or Down, position at handler's choice. Dog to be recalled to heel by handler, on command of judge or steward, whilst handler is walking away from dog, both to

continue forward until halted. The recall and halt points to be the same for each dog and handler. Test commences following handler's last command to dog. (15 points)

5. Retrieve a dumb—bell. Handlers may use their own dumb—bells. (20 points).

6. Sit one minute, handler in sight. (10 points)

7. Down five minutes, handler out of sight. (30 points)

8. Scent Discrimination, handler's scent on article. The total number of articles shall not exceed ten, all of which shall be clearly visible to the dog. (30 points)

Total 150 points

Class B – For dogs which have no won four prizes in Class B and open Class C in total. One command, by word or signal, except in Test 2. Extra commands or signals must be penalized.

1. Heel Free. The dog shall be required to walk at heel free and shall be tested at fast and slow pace. Each change of pace shall commence from the halt position. (30 points)

2. Send Away, Drop and Recall. On command of judge to handler, dog to be sent away in direction indicated by judge. After the dog has been dropped, handler will call the dog to heel whilst walking where directed by the judge and both will continue forward. No obstacle to be placed in the path of the dog. Simultaneous command and signal is permitted but as soon as the dog leaves the handler the arm must be dropped. (N.B. an extra command may be simultaneous command and signal, but an extra command must be penalized). (40 points)

3. Retrieve any one article provided by the judge but which must not be in any manner injurious to the dog (definitely excluding food or glass). The article to be picked up easily by any breed of dog in that Class and to be clearly visible to the dog. A separate similar article to be used for each dog. Test commences following Judge or Steward's words 'last command' to handler. (30 points).

4. Stand one minute, handler at least ten paces away from and facing away from the dog. (10 points)

5. Sit two minutes, handler out of sight. (20 points)

6. Down ten minutes, handler out of sight. (20 points)

7. Scent Discrimination, handler's scent on article provided by the judge. A separate similar article to be used for each dog and the total number of articles shall not exceed ten, all of which shall be clearly visible to the dog and shall be similar to the article given to the handler. Judges must use a separate similar scent decoy or decoys for each dog. No points will be awarded if the article is given to the dog. (30 points)

Total 180 points

Class C — At Championship Shows: for dogs which have won four first prizes in Class B or open Class C have gained 290 marks on no less than three occasions under three different judges in Open Class C and have been placed not lower than third on one occasion in Open Class C. Dogs which qualified for entry in Championship Class C prior to 1st May 1976 are also eligible.

At Open Shows: for dogs which have won four first prizes in Classes A or B in total.

At Limited and Sanction Shows: open to all dogs except Obedience Certificate winners and dogs which have obtained any award that counts towards the title of Obedience Champion or the equivalent thereof under the rules of any governing body recognized by the Kennel Club.

One command by word or signal, except in Test 2, where an extra command may be a simultaneous command and signal. Extra commands or signals must be penalized.

1. Heel Work. The dog shall be required to walk at heel free, and also be tested at fast and slow pace. At some time during this test, at the discretion of the judge, the dog shall be required, whilst walking to heel at normal pace, to be left at the Stand, Sit and Down in any order (the order to be the same for each dog) as and when directed by the judge. The handler shall continue forward alone, without hesitation, and continue as directed by the judge until he reaches his dog when both shall continue forward together until halted. Heel work may include left about turns and figure-of-eight at normal and/or slow pace. (60 points)

2. Send Away, Drop and Recall as in Class B. (40 points)

3. Retrieve any one article provided by the judge but which shall not be in any way injurious to the dog, as in Class B 3. (30 points)

4. Distant Control. Dog to Sit, Stand and Down at a marked place not less than ten paces from the handler, in any order on command from the judge to handler. Six instructions to be given in the same order for each dog. Excessive movement, i.e. more than one length of the dog, in any direction by the dog, having regard to its size, will be penalized. The dog shall start the exercise with its front feet behind a designated point. No penalty for excessive movement in a forward direction shall be imposed until the back legs of the dog pass the designated point. (50 points)

5. Sit two minutes, handler out of sight. (20 points)

6. Down ten minutes, handler out of sight. (50 points)

7. Scent Discrimination. Judge's scent on piece of marked cloth. Neutral and decoy cloths to be provided by the Show Executive. The judge shall not place his cloth in the ring himself, but it shall be placed by a steward. A separate similar piece to be used for each dog and the total number of separate similar pieces from which the dog shall discriminate shall not exceed ten. If a dog fetches or fouls a wrong article this must be replaced by a fresh article. At open-air shows all scent cloths must be adequately weighted to prevent them being blown about. The method of taking scent shall be at the handler's discretion but shall not require the judge to place his hand on, or lean towards the dog. A separate similar piece of cloth about 6 inches square but not more than 10 inches square shall be available to be used for giving each dog the scent. The judges should use a scent decoy or decoys. (50 points).

Total 300 points

The Kennel Club will offer an Obedience Certificate (Dog) and an Obedience Certificate (Bitch) for winners of First prizes in Class C Dog and Class C Bitch at a Championship Show, provided that the exhibits do not lose more than 10 points out of 300, and provided also that the Classes are open to all breeds.

Judges must also award a Reserve Best of Sex provided that the exhibit has not lost more than 10 points out of 300.

The Kennel Club will offer at Cruft's Dog Show each year the Kennel Club Obedience Championship – Bitch. A dog awarded one or more Obedience Cerificates during the calendar year preceding Cruft's show shall be entitled to compete.

The tests for the Championships shall be those required in Class C in these regulations. If the winning dog or bitch has lost more than 10 points out of 300, the Championship award shall be withheld.

As provided in Kennel Club Rule 4(c) the following dogs shall receive a Certificate to that effect from the Kennel Club:

(a) The winners of the Kennel Club Obedience Championships

(b) A dog awarded three Obedience Certificates under three different judges in accordance with these Regulations.

Explanatory Notes for Obedience Tests
(To be Read in Conjunction with Regulations S(2)

In all Classes the dog should work in a happy natural manner and prime consideration should be given to judging the dog and handler as a team. The dog may be encouraged and praised except where specifically stated otherwise. Instructions and commands to competitors may be made either by the judge or his steward by delegation.

In all tests the left hand side of a handler will be treated as the 'working side' unless the handler suffers from a physical disability and has the judges permission to work the dog on the right−hand side.

To signal the completion of each test the handler will be given the command 'test finished'.

It is permissible for handlers to practise their dogs before going to the ring provided there is no punitive correction and this is similar to an athlete limbering up before an event.

Timetable of Judging: To assist show executives the following guide timetable can be issued:

Class C: 6 dogs per hour
Class B: 8 dogs per hour
Class A: 12 dogs per hour
Beginner: 12 dogs per hour

The dog should be led into the ring for judging with a collar and lead attached (unless otherwise directed) and should be at the handler's side.

Heel on Lead : The dog should be sitting straight at the handler's side. On command the handler should walk briskly forward in a straight line with the dog at heel. The dog should be approximately level with and reasonably close to the handler's leg at all times when the handler is walking. The lead must be slack at all times. On the command 'left turn' or 'right turn' the handler should turn smartly at a right angle in the appropriate direction and the dog should keep its position at the handler's side. Unless otherwise directed, at the command 'about turn' the handler should turn about smartly on the spot through an angle of 180 degrees to the right and walk in the opposite direction, the dog maintaining its position at the handler's side. On the command 'halt' the handler should halt immediately and the dog should sit straight at the handler's side. Throughout this test the handler may not touch the dog or make use of the lead without penalty.

Heel Free: This test should be carried out in a similar manner as for Heel on Lead except that the dog must be off the lead throughout the test.

Retrieve a dumb−bell/article: At the start of this exercise the dog should be sitting at the handler's side. On command the handler must throw the dumb−bell/article in the direction indicated. The dog should remain at the Sit position until the handler is ordered to send it to retrieve the dumb−bell/article. The dog should move out promptly at a smart pace to collect the dumb−bell/article cleanly. It should return with it at a smart pace and sit straight in front of the

Millflash Danko
owned by Mrs S.Jeggo
(Photo: Diane Pearce)

Letton Premium
owned by Mrs Beck
(Photo: Diane Pearce)

85

handler. On command the handler should take the dumb—bell from the dog. On further command the dog should be sent to heel. In Classes A, B and C the test commences on the order 'last command' to handler.

Sit/Stay : The judge or steward will direct handlers to positions in the ring. The command 'last command' will be given when all are ready and handlers should then instantly give their last command to the dogs. Any further commands or signals to the dogs after this 'last command' will be penalized. Handlers will then be instructed to leave their dogs and walk to positions indicated until ordered to return to them. Dogs should remain at the Sit position throughout the test. This is a group test and all dogs must compete together. Time allowed for this test is at the judge's discretion.

Stand/Stay : This test should be carried out exactly as for the Sit/Stay except that dogs will be left in the Stand position throughout the test. This is a group test and all dogs must compete together.

Scent Discrimination : A steward will place the scented article amongst up to a maximum of nine other articles.

In a scent test if a dog brings in a wrong article or physically fouls any article i.e. mouths it: this article will be replaced.

The dog at this time should be facing away from the articles. On command the handler should bring the dog to a point indicated, give the dog scent and stand upright before sending the dog to find and retrieve the appropriate article. The dog should find the article and complete the test as for the Retrieve test. In all tests, scent articles are to be placed at least 2 feet apart. Limiting the time allowed for this test is at the judge's discretion.

Class A : Handler's scent on handler's article.

The judge should reject any articles he considers unfit by nature of their size, shape or substance and which in his opinion could have the effect of converting this elementary Scent Test into a Sight test. In this test at least one other article must be scented by someone other than the handler and the decoy article(s) must be similar for each dog.

Class B : Handler's scent on article provided by the judge.

The article must not be given to the dog. All articles must be separate and similar.

Class C : Judge's scent on piece of marked cloth. A decoy steward should not handle a cloth for a period longer than the judge.

Kennel Club Working Trial Regulations
S(1) 1st January 1975

Definitions of Stakes:

When entering for Championship or Open Working Trials, wins at Members Working Trials will not count.

No dog entered in P.D. or T.D. Stakes shall be eligible to enter in any other Stake at the meeting.

All Police dogs shall be considered qualified for entry in W.D. Championship Stakes if they hold the regional Police Dog qualification 'Excellent', provided that such entries are counter-signed by the Senior Police Officer I/C when such entries are made. Dogs holding this qualification are not eligible for entry in C.D. or U.D. Open or Championship Stakes, nor in W.D. Open Stakes.

No Working Trial Stake shall be limited to less than 30 dogs. If a limit is imposed on entries in any Stake, it shall be carried out by ballot after the date of closing for entries. Championship T.D. or P.D. Stakes shall not be limited by numbers in any way.

Open Working Trials:

Companion Dog (C.D.) Stake – For dogs which have not qualified C.D. Ex nor won three or more first prizes in C.D. Stakes or any prize in U.D. Stakes, W.D. Stakes, P.D. or T.D. Stakes at Open or Championship Working Trials.

All Breeds Utility (U.D.) Stake – For dogs which have not been awarded a Certificate of Merit in U.D., W.D., P.D., or T.D. Stakes.

Working Dog (W.D.) Stake – For dogs which have been awarded a Certificate of Merit in U.D. Stakes but not in W.D., P.D., or T.D. Stakes.

Tracking Dog (T.D.) Stake – For dogs which have been awarded a Certificate of Merit in W.D. Stakes.

Police Dog (P.D.) Stake – For dogs which have been awarded a Certificate of Merit in W.D. Stakes.

Championship Working Trials:

Companion Dog (C.D.) Stake – For dogs which have not won three or more first prizes in C.D. Stakes or any prize in any other Stake at Championship Working Trials.

All Breeds Utility (U.D.) Stake – For dogs which have won a Certificate of Merit in a U.D. Stake. A dog is not eligible for entry in this Stake if it has been entered in the W.D. Stake on the same day.

Working Dog (W.D.) Stake – For dogs which have qualified U.D. Ex and have won a Certificate of Merit in W.D. Stakes.

Tracking Dog (T.D.) Stake – For dogs which have qualified W.D. Ex and which have won a Certificate of Merit at Open Trials in T.D. Stakes.

Police Dog (P.D.) Stake – For dogs which have qualified W.D. Ex or have won a Certificate of Merit in P.D. Stakes.

Any dog qualified for U.D., W.D., T.D., or P.D. Stakes at the 28th February 1969 is still eligible for entry in those Stakes.

Schedule of Points

Companion Dog (C.D.) Stake
Description of Exercises and Individual Marks

Group 1 – Heelwork

1. Heel on Leash. (5 points)
On the handler's command 'Heel', the dog should follow as closely as possible to the left knee of the handler, who should walk smartly in his normal and natural manner. Any tightening or jerking of the leash, or any act, signal or command which, in the opinion of the Judges gives the dog unnecessary or unfair assistance, shall be penalized. The exercise shall consist of 'left turns', 'about turns', and marching in the 'figure of eight' at normal walking pace between objects or people two yards apart. The Judge may, at his discretion, test also at a fast or very slow pace.

2. Heel Free. (15 points)
This should be executed as in No. 1 except that the dog is off the leash.

Group Total 20 Points.

Group 11 – Control

3.   Sit (two minutes). (10 points)
The dogs shall sit for the full period of two minutes, all the handlers being out of sight as far as possible from the dogs at the Judge's discretion. On the handlers' return to their dogs the latter should not move from the sitting position until the Judge's permission has been given. All dogs shall be tested together, sufficient Stewards being detailed to assist. The Judges may cause the dogs to be tested by sending Stewards to walk among them during the exercise.

4.   Recall to Handler. (10 points)
The dog should be recalled from the 'down' or sitting position, the handler being as far as possible from the dog at the discretion of the Judge. The dog should return at a smart pace and sit in front of the handler, afterwards going smartly to heel on command or signal; handler to await command of the Judge.

5.   Sending the dog away. (10 points)
In the direction indicated by the Judge not less than 20 yards (18m.) and dropping on order from Judge to handler. The dog should drop instantly and remain down until the Judge instructs the handler to call his dog up.

6.   Down 10 minutes, handler out of sight. (10 points)
The dog must remain in the lying down position for the full period specified, the handler being out of sight until ordered to return by the Judge. The dog should not rise from the 'down' position until the Judge declares the exercise complete. The Judge may cause a dog to be tested by sending Stewards to walk around it during the exercise.

Group Total 40 points.
Minimum Group Qualifying Mark 28 points.

Group 111 – Agility

7.
(a) Scale jump (3), Stay (2), and recall over scale (5). (10 points)
Dogs not exceeding 10-ins. at shoulder 3-ft.
Dogs not exceeding 15-ins. at shoulder 4-ft.
Dogs exceding 15-ins. at should 6-ft.
(b) Clear jump. (5 points)
Dogs not exceeding 10-ins. at shoulder 1-ft.6-ins.
Dogs not exceeding 15-ins. at shoulder 2-ft.
Dogs exceeding 15-ins. at shoulder 3-ft.
(c) Long jump. (5 points)
Dogs not exceeding 10-ins. at shoulder 4-ft.
Dogs not exceeding 15-ins. at shoulder 6-ft.
Dogs exceeding 15-ins. at shoulder 9-ft.

Group Total 20 Points.
Minimum Group Qualifying Mark 14 points.

Group 1V – Retrieving and Nose

8. Retrieving a dumb-bell on the flat. (10 points)
The dog shall not move forward to retrieve nor deliver to hand on return until ordered by the handler on the Judge's instructions. The retrieve should be executed at a fast trot or gallop without mouthing or playing with the object. After delivery the dog should return to heel.

9. Elementary search. (10 points)
Controlled search of an area of foiled ground to find and retrieve one Judge's article with handler's scent, placed by a Steward, unseen by dog and handler. This area should be approximately 12 yards (10.9m.) square and the time allowed 2 minutes. A separate area to be used for each dog. Handler must remain outside the area although allowed to move.

Group Total 20 points.
Minimum Group Qualifying Mark 14 points.

Total Points 100.
Minimum Group Qualifying Mark 70 points.

All Breeds Utility Dog (U.D.) Stake
Description of Exercises and Individual Marks

Group 1 – Control

1. Heel free. (5 points)
2. Sending dog away not less than 20 yards (18.2m.) and dropping on order from Judge to handler. (10 points)
3. Retrieving dumb-bell of handler's choice on the flat. (5 points)
4. Long down (10 minutes), handler out of sight. (10 points)
5. Steadiness to gunshot. (5 points)

Group Total 35 Points
Minimum Group Qualifying Mark 25 points.

Group 11 – Agility

6.
(a) Scale (3), Stay (2), and recall over scale (5). (10 points)
Dogs not exceeding 10-ins. at shoulder 3-ft.
Dogs not exceeding 15-ins. at shoulder 4-ft.
Dogs exceeding 15-ins. at shoulder 6-ft.
(b) Clear jump. (5 points)
Dogs not exceeding 10-ins. at shoulder 1-ft.6-ins.
Dogs not exceeding 15-ins. at shoulder 2-ft.
Dogs exceeding 15-ins. at shoulder 3-ft.
(c) Long jump. (5 points)

Dogs not exceeding 10-ins. at shoulder 4-ft.
Dogs not exceeding 15-ins. at shoulder 6-ft.
Dogs exceeding 15-ins. at shoulder 9-ft.

Group Total 20 Points.
Minimum Group Qualifying Mark 14 points.

Group 111 – Nosework

7.   Search – Controlled search of an area of foiled ground to find and retrieve four strange articles handled and placed by some person other than the handler. The area should be fresh for each dog and approximately 25 yards square (22.8m.) and the time allowed five minutes. Two articles must be found (see item F in the 'Notes for the Guidance of Judges and Competitors'). (35 points)

8.   Leash track – Not less than half a mile (0.8m.) long and at least half an hour old on track laid as far as possible by a stranger to the dog. The tracklayer's article to be left at the end of the track. One peg, not more than 30 yards (27.4m.) from the commencement of the tract will be left to indicate the direction of the track.

   One recast will be allowed at the discretion of the Judge (see item 1 (a) in 'Notes for the Guidance of Judges and Competitors').

For the track. (95 points)
For recognition of article by the dog. (15 points)

Group Total 145 Points.
Minimum Group Qualifying Mark 102 points.

Total Points 200.
Minimum Group Qualifying Mark 141 points.

Working Dog (W.D.) Stake
Description of Exercises and Individual Marks

Group 1 – Control

1.   Heel free. (5 points)
2.   Sending dog away not less than 20 yards (18.2m.) and dropping on order from Judge to handler. (10 points)
3.   Retrieving dumb-bell of handler's choice on the flat. (5 points)
4.   Long down (10 minutes), handler out of sight. (10 points)
5.   Steadiness to gunshot. (5 points)

Group Total 35 Points.
Minimum Group Qualifying Mark 25 points.

Group 11 – Agility

6.
(a) 6-ft. (1.8m.) Scale (3), Stay (2), and recall over scale (5). (10 points)
(b) Clear jump 3-ft. (0.9m.). (5 points)
(c) Long jump 9-ft. (2.7m.). (5 points)

Group Total 20 Points.
Minimum Group Qualifying Mark 14 points.

Group 111 – Nosework

7.   Search – Controlled search of an area of foiled ground to find and retrieve four strange articles handled and placed by some person other than the handler. The area should be fresh for each dog and approximately 25 yards (22.8m.) square, and the time allowed five minutes. Two articles must be found (see item F in the 'Notes for the Guidance of Judges and Competitors'). (35 points)

8.   Leash track – There should be no recasts on the direction of the Judge. The track shall be not less than half a mile long and at least one and a half hours old. Two different kinds of article will be dropped on the track, similar articles to be used by each tracklayer and readily identifiable by him. One article must be found to qualify. (See item 1 (b) in 'Notes for the Guidance of Judges and Competitors').

For the track. (80 points)
For recognition of two articles by the dog (15 points each). (30 points)

Group Total 145 Points.
Minimum Group Qualifying Mark 102 points.

Total Points 200.
Minimum Group Qualifying Mark 141 points.
Tracking Dog (T.D.) Stake
Description of Exercises and Individual Marks

Group 1 – Control

1.   Heel free. (5 points)
2.   Down (10 minutes), handler out of sight. (10 points)
3.   Directional control. Sending dog away in direction indicated by the Judge not less than 50 yards (45.7m.). Stopping and redirecting not less than 20 yards (18.2m.). (10 points)
4.   Speak and cease speaking on command. (5 points)
5.   Steadiness to gunshot. (5 points)

Group Total 35 Points.
Minimum Group Qualifying Mark 25 points.

Group 11 – Agility

6.
(a) 6-ft. (1.8m.) Scale (3), Stay (2), and recall over scale (5). (10 points)
(b) Clear jump 3-ft. (0.9m.). (5 points)
(c) Long jump 9-ft. (2.7m.). (5 points)

Group Total 20 Points.
Minimum Group Qualifying Mark 14 points.

Group 111 – Nosework

7.   Search – Controlled search of an area of foiled ground to find and retrieve four strange articles handled and placed by some person other than the handler. The area should be fresh for each dog and approximately 25 yards (22.8m.) square, and the time allowed five minutes. Two articles must be found (se item F in the 'Notes for the Guidance of Judges and Competitors'). (35 points)

8.   Leash track – There shall be no recasts on the direction of the Judge. The track shall be not less than half a mile (0.8Km.) long and at least three hours old. Three different kinds of article will be dropped on the track, similar articles to be used by each tracklayer and readily identifiable by him. A dog must find two articles to qualify (see Working Trial Regulation No.8).

For the track. (100 points)
For recognition of three articles (10 points each). (30 points)

Group Total 165 Points.
Minimum Group Qualifying Mark 155 points.

CHAPTER 6

Exhibiting

Dog exhibiting is a popular pastime today in most lands where the pedigree dog has established himself. It is an interesting hobby, and one which many German Shepherd Dog owners have taken up in recent years.

A champion's title is the aim of the ambitious and experienced exhibitor. The newcomer to the show ring will have to be content with more modest activities: a number of different types of show are available from which he can choose. There are Breed Shows, in which he will compete against other German Shepherd Dogs and there are Any Variety events, in which the classes are usually made up of different breeds competing on their respective merits against each other. The former are of course more popular, as every German Shepherd owner likes to know how his dog compares with another German Shepherd. This is the judge's job to place the dogs one, two, three and so on in order of merit, according to his opinion — that is what counts on that day at least. The next week, another judge with the same dogs before him may reverse or revise the placings, because he will be judging according to *his* opinion. This is why dog shows continue; if every judge did the same thing, that is, put the same dog first, the same second, and so on, everyone would become bored and give up the game. It is the atmosphere of chance coupled with competition which makes dog showing so interesting and brings more and more devotees to its ranks.

The other type of show, in which you exhibit your German Shepherd's good points against those of another breed's or other breeds', is rather different. The judge is supposed to know all about the breeds he has before him and then after judging them, to pick out the best three or four for prizes. That sometimes the element of chance involved in this procedure is high goes without saying, and exhibiting at such shows, especially when the classes are well filled, is more of a 'game'. However, they do offer a form of training in show procedure for novice dogs and novice owners, and in the absence of German Shepherd Dog specialist shows they should be patronized. Often enough, the fine upstanding and elegant German Shepherd Dog by his very presence and beauty will 'stand out' in the show ring and be chosen as winner !

Ch.Leo of Llanyraven
owned by Mrs N.Evans
(Photo: Diane Pearce)

Kenmils Preciosa
owned by
Mr B.Broadbank
(Photo: Diane Pearce)

It is at this point that a newcomer to the show ring has to be on his guard. It is easy, following such an unexpected win (one 'out of the bag' so to speak), to become tremendously enthusiastic, cast all caution to the wind and go out and buy three or four new dogs to start a breeding kennel! This may seem exaggerated but older breeders will know that it has happened and it goes on happening in every breed. The trouble is that so often the dog–show game, at first an exhilarating pastime, can become almost at once a business imbued with rivalry and jealousy. No novice should wax too keen with his dog until it has become established that he has a good and promising exhibit. He should maintain a stable attitude to his dogs and the exhibition world, avoiding the coteries and cliques which abound in most competitive circles and undoubtedly exist in dogdom. By doing so, he will enjoy German Shepherds and the company of his friends in the breed, one which is noted for its camaraderie and comparative freedom from the ringside gossip which seems to beset so many worthy breeds.

Ch.Lucille of Keyna
owned by Miss Z.Pearce
(Photo: Diane Pearce)

Ch.Olivia of Eveley
owned by
Mrs M.Tidbold
(Photo: Diane Pearce)

Hendrawens
Easter Bonnet
owned by Mrs A.Ringwald
(Photo: Diane Pearce)

Kenmils Romantique
owned by Mrs G.Uglione
(Photo: Diane Pearce)

The Different Shows in Great Britain

Exemption

Exemption is a very small event, usually held in conjunction with a holiday-time fete and judged by some notability who may or may not know much about dogs. You can enter at this type of show without registering your dog at the Kennel Club, but this body's disciplinary rules nevertheless have to be observed. Only four classes for pedigree dogs may be scheduled in which the breeds are judged according to their breed Standards, but the classes fall into the Any Variety category and no specialist breed classes will be found. The remaining classes are, for want of a better word, termed 'novelty' classes, and in these mongrels and cross−breds can compete. Such classes as 'dog in best condition', 'dog with the most soulful eyes' and suchlike prove very popular with the public, but any win at such a show must be taken in very light vein.

Sanction and Limited

The Sanction Show has for a long time been regarded as an ideal training ground for up−and−coming exhibitors. This type of show is also used extensively by noted breeding kennels to bring out youngsters and yearlings with Championship promise. Consequently, the true novice with a German Shepherd he wants to try out can easily find himself 'swamped' with the *creme-de-la-creme* around him. It is advisable to enter in perhaps three classes when attending such a show. The Puppy and Maiden classes are usually well filled with mixed breeds, but a striking variety such as the German Shepherd stands a reasonably good chance of getting into the first three awards, provided he is a good specimen of course. He may have an even better chance than he would have in a breed class at the same show with six or seven entrants. These matters need to be assessed, and the recruit to the exhibition world will soon learn by experience in which classes he stands the most chance of winning. The Limited Show, so called because entry is limited to a certain number of classes, can be assessed in a similar manner. Both types of show are restricted or confined to the members of the club or society promoting the event and Challenge Certificate winners are not eligible.

Open

The Open type of show can be benched or otherwise as the promoters and/or the Kennel Club see fit. Often they are held in conjunction with an Agricultural Show or County Show and are frequently open−air events. Conditions are similar to those enforced at a Championship Show, but no Challenge Certificates are available. At the open air all−breed events, competition in the breeds is often sparse, and many exhibits of less than average worth can come away with important prize awards. However, if the Open Show is organized by a breed society such as The Alsatian League then the best in the breed will be on show and competition will probably be fierce.

Championship

Championship Shows are benched events. These are the most important shows and they are always well attended as Challenge Certificates are on offer (as a rule), and these are avidly sought by exhibitors. Sometimes these shows will run for two, even three, days, although the Working Group into which German Shepherds fall will be judged on only one of these days. Cruft's Dog Show schedules almost every variety and offers Challenge Certificates to most. Some experienced exhibitors aver that it is just as easy to win at a Championship Show as it is to take an award at a mere Sanction Show. Most judges will agree that this is often true and will be able to recall instances when they have been confronted with dogs at Championship Shows which have gone into the prize awards and which they had previously been unable to place at a Sanction Show !

The question is — what sort of show should you attend when you are a novice? I favour breed classes above any other sort, and German Shepherds are usually well catered for because most show managements only put on breeds which are likely to bring them in a profit or at least enable them to break even. The German Shepherd Dog clubs are well aware of this situation and guarantee classes at important events in an effort not only to publicize the breed but also to encourage owners and breeders to exhibit. Every German Shepherd Dog owner ought to join his local specialist club and support shows in which the breed is scheduled. If you love the breed you will want to see it thrive and develop. The Limited Shows are perhaps preferable to Sanction Shows because the latter permit the entry of mature German Shepherds, some of which may well have done a good deal of winning and represent insurmountable competition for the youngster being tried out. Open Shows also offer the novice exhibitor a sound opportunity, for again he will find Puppy, Maiden, and Novice classes in which he can try his hand against dogs who are probably no better or no worse than he. There is a trend in many societies to put on Beginners' and Special Beginners' classes in the various breeds; this is to be applauded, for many new owners need encouragement in the general world of dogs.

The Match

The match is conducted under Kennel Club Rules and Regulations. It is a competition on the 'knock-out' system between pairs of dogs, whether of the same breed or invited breeds. The main purpose of the Match is to interest and educate club members. A small prize is usually awarded to the winner.

If you plan to make a hobby of dog-showing, read the rules not only of the club or society where you plan to exhibit but the Kennel Club Rules and Regulations too. These are quite rigid and will be strictly enforced, for dog—exhibiting has been brought to a high level of procedure by the Kennel Club which, since it was founded in 1873, has eliminated the many malpractices of the early days and now controls the breeding and exhibition of dogs.

Preparing for the Show

To make any real impact at your first show you must at least try to present your dog in such a way that his good points will be effectively displayed and he will parade with a fine degree of deportment. This means not only that the dog himself must be trained to show but that you may have to give yourself a modicum of training too. A dog and his handler are in effect very little different from a theatrical 'double act'. Both play an important part in the effort to achieve success – in this case a first prize and later, who knows, a Challenge Certificate. Consequently, both dog and handler need to be on their toes, as things do not rest entirely with the dog and his points but also with the way they are presented.

Being a big animal, the German Shepherd Dog is not particularly easy to manoeuvre or place standing. However, if you have had him since he was a puppy and started training him when he was four or five months old, there will be an understanding between you, and he will readily interpret the merest twist of your wrist on his leash and respond at once. If this ideal state does not exist then you must start at once to train your exhibit towards this end. For instance, he must be taught to enter the ring elegantly and confidently so that the judge may assess the value of his general appearance. No judge appreciates a lunging or hang-back exhibit, and any German Shepherd entering the ring in either way will almost certainly lose points before he starts. The dog must be taught to stand firm at command, preferably in profile to the judge so that the beauty of his outline can be appreciated. If an exhibit is inclined to reveal certain faults in his make-up by posing this way, then the handler must learn to employ certain subtleties in his method of presentation so as to obscure or disguise them. To do this is perfectly legitimate and is an art in itself.

In effect your must learn to handle your dog and show him to the judge by displaying his best points. If he has some bad points (and few dogs have not), keep them from the judge's eye as much as you can. If he is a clever judge he will find them quickly enough, but then only a certain percentage are 'clever' judges.

Most shows are unbenched, so it behoves you to find yourself a cosy place somewhere in the hall where you will remain undisturbed until you are ready to exhibit. Corners where you can keep your dog under control and stop inquisitive dogs from poking their noses too closely are best. Lay down a cheap blanket and install yourself and the dog until the first class in which you are entered becomes due.

The First Class

Soon you will hear your ring number called. You will know the number you hold because it will appear in the show catalogue against your dog's name. You will be told where to place yourself and your exhibit by the ring stewards, of which there are usually two, helping and supporting the judge. Their job is to usher in the exhibits as the various classes become due and in effect to keep an eye on the orderly running of the ring. Once all the class exhibits are present and standing ready, the judge will commence judging. He will probably beckon you over to him and ask you to stand your dog in front of him. This you will do, and he will run his hands over the dog and start to assess his virtues and quality. All this time you will be taking care that the dog stands firm and square and behaves himself. The judge will want to look in his mouth and examine his teeth, gums and jaw formation. He may do this himself or may require you to open up your dog's mouth for him.

Once he has gone over the dog, he may want to assess his movement and ask you to walk your exhibit up and down or around the ring. He can then see the quality of his rear action as the dog moves away. He will note the musculature and general features of the exhibit's gait and will probably get some good idea of the animal's soundness and stamp of breed. As you return to him he will see the dog's forward action, front, poise and balance and will also note the breed type possessed by your exhibit. You may then be asked (with some of the other exhibits) to circle the ring. This will give the judge an opportunity to view the dog in profile and to see how he steps out, his leg and shoulder action, rear angulation, and also his balance. Make sure that your dog moves with style, elegance and breed quality. This means that he must move freely. The leash must be held slack yet should keep the dog in complete control. Make sure that he does not sniff too closely at the dog in front of him and that his speed is calculated to show his points to best advantage. Do not worry if your dog evinces a little flamboyance. This is never a bad thing in the show ring. A canine 'show−off' in the ring gets away with a lot and often covers up some of his bad

Ardra Willow of
Timberdown
owned by
Mrs S.Thompson
(Photo: Diane Pearce)

Australian Champion
Marlish Granmaster
owned by
Mr J.Sherri
(Photo: Diane Pearce)

WT.Ch.Greyvalley Grock
(Photo: Dog World)

WT.Ch.Greyvalley Grock
(Photo: Dog World)

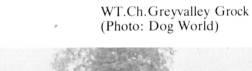

WT.Ch.Bois of Limbrook
winner of PD Stakes   a.S.P.A.D.S.October 1975

(Photo: Dog World)

points in his type and make—up. A dog can carry on a long time just 'looking' good, but eventually a perceptive judge will find out if he really *is* good. This is why the dogs who *look* good and are *really* good become the big winners. Those who do not merit full marks in both respects seldom make the grade. Poor ones fall heavily by the wayside in the course of their careers, no matter how well campaigned and advertised they have been. This is because German Shepherd Dogs are established in a closer circle than is the case in many other breeds, and although competition in the breed is fairly weighty numerically it is also quite fierce in respect of quality, and individuals are judged closely and discussed intimately. Consequently, any weaknesses in a dog's make—up are sought out more quickly and revealed sooner than in some other breeds.

Once the judge has decided which dog he prefers for first prize (red card) he will probably place it out in the centre of the ring facing the main body of spectators. Then other dogs will be selected to fill second (blue card), third (yellow card), and reserve (green card) places. Assuming that the judge is satisfied with his placings the steward will then receive his instructions to distribute the award cards. Always be on your guard right up to the last moment of judging and keep your dog on his toes, displaying himself to best advantage. It is not unusual for a judge to change his mind just before the prizes are given and alter his placings. It can be a disappointment not to win, but to have a prize cancelled or curtailed right at the moment of triumph can be quite desolating, especially if it was a result of personal failure in ringcraft tactics.

Future Showing

Assuming that you have become an enthusiast and intend to continue exhibiting you will in due course have to consider the competition in big Championship Shows. If your dog is just an average specimen you are unlikely to get to the top with him — a champion's title is for the super dog, and no judge should ever award a dog a Challenge Certificate unless he is convinced that the exhibit is worthy of that title. There maybe cases in which dogs of rather less than top quality have achieved their titles mainly because of clever campaigning on the part of their owners. Fortunately such cases are rare — they do no good, even harm, to the breed, and the dogs involved are seldom accepted and/or bred to in normal circumstances. The really good dog usually makes the grade, however, provided his owner does not give up or become too disillusioned half way through the dog's career. Exhibiting needs enthusiasm, dedication, and deter-mination in no small measure, especially if a champion's title is the aim . For this three Challenge Certificates awarded by three different judges are needed; one of the Challenge Certificates must have been awarded after the dog has become twelve months of age.

Championship Shows are benched events. The benches are galvanized three sided pens which accommodate the dogs while they are not actually being exhibited in the show ring. Every dog has its catalogue number affixed above its head on the bench, and this allows visitors to the show to inspect the exhibits at will. You will require a bench chain, and it is also a good idea to have a blanket or rug on which the dog can rest. One end of the bench chain is affixed to the dog's collar and the other end is passed through a ring set into the rear of the bench and then clipped to the chain itself, according to the freedom you wish to allow your dog on his bench. It is wise to permit him just enough room to make himself comfortable, curl up, and go to sleep. If you can, take a quick look at his neighbouring competitors. If they seem placid, well and good, but if one appears nervous adjust the chain so that your dog's nose does not project beyond the extremities of the dividing panel. It is better to be safe than sorry.

As this type of show is usually a full–day affair and you are confined there, win or lose, you should come well prepared. This means food and drink for the dog (the food must not be given him until *after* he has been judged), similar supplies for yourself, and enough suitable vessels to administer them. It is a good idea to have a pocket first–aid kit, but never forget the tit–bits, so important to the average exhibit, and also the grooming tools. With all these things you should be well set for the day ahead. It is to be hoped that you will do your share of winning and collect a few prize cards. If you manage to win your first or second Challenge Certificate you will be happy indeed, but remember – it is the third and final one which makes your dog a champion that is the hardest and most worrying to get – at least, this is what so many exhibitors say!

Registering Your Dog

All German Shepherd Dogs should be registered at the Kennel Club. The current Schedule of fees is available from them on request and anyone requiring information or guidance should write to the Secretary of the Kennel Club at 1-4 Clarges Street, Piccadilly, London W1Y 8AB, Telephone 01 493 6651

The American Kennel Club

Today the German Shepherd Dog is a major breed in the United States and has good attendances at the leading shows. The American system of defining and classifying shows is given below in extracts from the American Kennel Club's Rules Applying to Registration and Dog Shows. These are reproduced with the kind permission of the American Kennel Club.

American Kennel Club Schedule of Fees

Litter Registration, each $7.00
Individual Dog Registration, each $4.00
Change of ownership, each $4.00
Certified pedigree (3 Generations) each $5.00
ditto.(4 Generations) each $10.00
The Complete Dog Book $7.95
Pure Bred Dogs ¶ *American Kennel Gazette,* Single copy $2.00
Subscription rates
1 year $10.00
2 years $18
3 years $25.00
Canadian and Foreign postage extra $2.00
Stud Book Register, single copy $2.00
Stud Book Register, 1 year $18.00
Foreign postage extra : $2.00
Duplicate Certificate of Registration $4.00
Duplicate Championship Certificate $3.00
Duplicate Breeders Certificate $2.00
Duplicate C.D.,C.D.X.,U.D.,and T.D. Certificates $2.00
Single copies of the *Rules Applying to Registration and Dog Shows, Registration and Field Trials, Beagle Field Trial Rules and Obedience Regulations are available at no charge on individual request.*
The address of the American Kennel Club is:
The American Kennel Club Inc.,
51 Madison Avenue.,
New York, N.Y.10010

American Kennel Club Dog Shows Defined

Section 1. A member show is a show at which championship points may be awarded, given by a club or association which is a member of The American Kennel Club.

Section 2. A licences show is a show at which championship points may be awarded, given by a club or association which is not a member of The American Kennel Club but which has been specially licenced by The American Kennel Club to give the specific show designated in the licence.

Section 3. A member or licenced all—breed club may apply to the AKC for approval to hold a show at which championship points may be awarded with entries restricted to puppies that are eligible for entry in the regular puppy class and dogs that have been placed first, second or third in a regular class at a show at which championship points were awarded, provided the club submitting such an application has held at least one show annually for at least ten years immediately prior to the year in which application for a show so restricted is made, and further provided that there shall not have been less than 900 dogs entered in its show (or in one of its shows if the club holds more than one show a year) in the year preceding the year in which application is made for its first show with entries so restricted.

When an application for this type of restricted entry show has been approved by the AKC the only dogs eligible for entry shall be puppies that are eligible for entry in the regular puppy class and those dogs that have been placed first, second of third in a regular class at a show at which championship points were awarded held not less than sixty days prior to the first day of the show at which entries will be so restricted.

However, a club making application to hold a show restricted to entries of dogs as specified above may further restrict entries by excluding all puppies or all puppies six months and under nine months and/or by excluding dogs that have been placed third or dogs that have been placed second and third, provided the extent of these further restrictions are specified on the application.

Any club whose application has been approved to hold a show with restricted entries as described in this section shall indicate the extent of the restrictions in its premium list.

Section 4. A member or licenced all-breed club may apply to the AKC for approval to hold a show at which championship points will be awarded with entries restricted to dogs that are champions on the records of the AKC and dogs that have been credited with one or more championship points, provided the club submitting the application has held at least one show annually for at least 15 years immediately prior to the year in which application for a show so restricted is made, and further provided that there shall not be less than 1200 dogs entered in its show (or in one of its shows if the club holds more than one show a year) in the year preceding the year in which application for its first show with entries so restricted is made.

When an application for this type of restricted entry show has been approved by the AKC, the only dogs eligible for entry shall be those dogs that have been recorded as champions and those dogs that have been credited with one or more championship points as a result of competition at shows held not less than 60 days prior to the first day of the show at which entries will be so restricted.

However, a club making application to hold a show restricted to entries of dogs as specified above, may further restrict entries by excluding all puppies or all puppies six months and under nine months and/or by excluding dogs that have not been credited with at least one major championship point rating, provided the extent of these further restrictions are specified on the application.

Any club whose application has been approved to hold a show with restricted entries as described in this section shall indicate the extent of the restrictions in its premium list.

Section 5. A member or licenced show with a limited entry, at which champion—ship points may be awarded may be given by a club or association in the event said club or association considers it necessary to *limit* the *total entry* at its show due to the limitations of space. The total number of entries to be accepted together with the reason therefor, must be indicated on the cover or title page of the *premium list* A specified closing date, in accordance with Chapter 9 Section 9 must be indicated in the premium list together with a statement that entries will close on said date or when the limit has been reached, if prior thereto. No entries can be accepted, cancelled or substituted after the entry is closed. The specified closing date shall be used in determining whether a dog is eligible for the Novice Classes at the show.

Section 6 A specialty show is a show given by a club or association formed for the improvement of any one breed of pure—bred dogs, at which championship points may be awarded to said breed.

Section 7. An American—bred specialty show is a show for American—bred dogs only, given by a member club or association formed for the improvement of any one breed of pure—bred dogs at which championship points may be awarded to said breed.

Section 8. A sanctioned match is an informal meeting at which pure—bred dogs may compete but not for championship points, held by a club or association whether or not a member of the AKC by obtaining the sanction of the AKC.

American Kennel Club Dog Show Classifications

Section 1. The following breeds and/or varieties of breeds, divided by groups, shall be all the breeds and/or varieties of breeds for which regular classes of the AKC may be provided at any show held under AKC rules. The Board of Directors may either add to, transfer from one group to another, or delete from said list of breeds and/or varieties of breeds, whenever in its opinion registrations of such breed and/or variety in the Stud Book justify such action.

GROUP 1 SPORTING DOGS
Pointers
Pointers (German Shorthaired)
Pointers (German Wirehaired)
Retrievers (Chesapeake Bay)
Retrievers (Curly-coated)
Retrievers (Flat−coated)
Retrievers (Golden)
Retrievers (Labrador)
Setters (English)
Setters (Gordon)
Spaniels (American Water)
Spaniels (Brittany)
Spaniels (Clumber)
Spaniels (Cocker)
Three varieties: Solid color, Black. Solid color other than black, including black and tan. Parti-color.
Spaniels (English Cocker)
Spaniels (English Springer)
Spaniels (Field)
Spaniels (Irish Water)
Spaniels (Sussex)
Spaniels (Welsh Springer)
Vizslas
Weimaraners
Wirehaired Pointing Griffons

GROUP 2 HOUNDS

Afghan Hounds
Basenjis
Basset Hounds
Beagles
Two varieties : Not exceeding 13 inches in height. Over 13 inches in height but not exceeding 15 inches in height.
Black and Tan Coonhounds
Bloodhounds
Borzois
Dachshunds
Three varieties: Longhaired. Smooth. Wirehaired.
Foxhounds (American)
Foxhounds (English)
Greyhounds
Harriers
Irish Wolfhounds
Norwegian Elkhounds
Otter Hounds
Rhodesian Ridgebacks
Salukis
Scottish Deerhounds
Whippets

GROUP 3 WORKING DOGS

Alaskan Malamutes
Belgian Malinois
Belgian Sheepdogs
Belgian Tervuren
Bernese Mountain Dogs
Bouviers Des Flandres
Boxers
Briards
Bullmastiffs
Collies
   Two varieties : Rough. Smooth.
Dobermann Pinschers

German Shepherd Dogs
Giant Schnauzers
Great Danes
Great Pyrenees
Komondorok
Kuvaszov
Mastiffs
Newfoundlands
Old English Sheepdogs
Pulik
Rottweilers
St.Bernards
Samoyeds
Shetland Sheepdogs
Siberian Huskies
Standard Schnauzers
Welsh Corgis
Welsh Corgis (Cardigan)
Welsh Corgis (Pembroke)

GROUP 4 TERRIERS

Airedale Terriers
American Staffordshire Terriers
Australian Terriers
Bedlington Terriers
Border Terriers
Bull Terriers
   Two varieties : White. Colored
Cairn Terriers
Dandie Dinmont Terriers
Fox Terriers
   Two varieties : Smooth. Wire
Irish Terriers
Kerry Blue Terriers
Lakeland Terriers
Manchester Terriers
   Two varieties: Standard, over 12 pounds and not exceeding 22 pounds. Toy
   (in Toy group)

Miniature Schnauzers
Norwich Terriers
Scottish Terriers
Sealyham Terriers
Skye Terriers
Welsh Terriers
West Highland White Terriers

GROUP 5 TOYS

Affenpinschers
Brussels Griffons
Chihuahuas
  Two varieties ; Smooth Coat. Long Coat
English Toy Spaniels
  Two varieties : King Charles and Ruby. Blenheim and Prince Charles
Italian Greyhounds
Japanese Spaniels
Maltese
Manchester Terriers
  Two varieties : Toy; not exceeding 12 pounds. Standard (in Terrier Group)
Miniature Pinschers
Papillons
Pekingese
Pomeranians
Poodle
  Three varieties: Toy; not exceeding 10 inches. Miniature (in Non-sporting group). Standard (in Non-sporting group)
Pugs
Shih Tzu
Silky Terriers
Yorkshire Terriers

GROUP 6 NON-SPORTING DOGS

Boston Terriers
Bulldogs
Chow Chows
Dalmatians

French Bulldogs
Keeshonden
Lhasa Apsos
Poodles
  Three varieties : Miniature, over 10 inches and not exceeding 15 inches
  Standard, over 15 inches. Toy (in Toy group)
Schipperkes

Section 2. No class shall be provided for any dog under six months of age except at sanctioned matches when approved by the AKC.

Section 3. The regular classes of the AKC shall be as follows:
  Puppy
  Novice
  Bred−by−exhibitor
  American−bred
  Open
  Winners

Section 4. The Puppy Class shall be for dogs that are six months of age and over, but under twelve months. That were whelped in the United States of America or Canada, and that are not champions. The age of the dog shall be calculated up to and inclusive of the day of the show. For example a dog whelped January 1st is eligible to compete in a puppy class show the first day of which is July 1st the same year and may continue to compete in puppy classes at shows up to an including the 31st day of December of the same year, but is not eligible to compete in a puppy class at a show the first day of which is January 1st of the following year.

Section 5. The Novice Class shall be for dogs six months of age and over, whelped in the United States of America or Canada, which have not, prior to the date of closing of entries, won three first prizes in the Novice Class, a first prize in Bred-by-Exhibitor, American-bred, or Open Classes, nor one or more points towards their championships.

Section 6. The Bred−by−Exhibitor Class shall be for dogs whelped in the United States of America, or, if individually registered in the AKC Stud Book, for dogs whelped in Canada, that are six months of age or over, that are not champions, and that are owned wholly or in part by the person or the spouse of the person who was the breeder or one of the breeders of record.

Ch.Gorsefield Shah
owned by Messrs
Pilling and Moore
(Photo: Diane Pearce)

Ch.Norwulf Enchantment
owned by Mrs M.Darron
(Photo: Diane Pearce)

Squaredeal Loki
owned by Miss B.Lambert
(Photo: Diane Pearce)

Novem Etude
owned by
Mrs S.H.Roberts
(Photo: Diane Pearce)

Dogs entered in this class must be handled in the class by an owner or by a member of the immediate family of the owner.

For purposes of this section, the members of an immediate family are: husband, wife, father, mother, son, daughter, brother, sister.

Section 7. The American-bred Class shall be for all dogs (except champions) six months of age or over, whelped in the United States of America, by reason of a mating which took place in the United States of America.

Section 8. The Open Class shall be for any dog six months of age or over except in a member specialty club show held only for American–bred dogs, in which case the Open Class shall be only for American–bred dogs.

Section 9. The Winners Class, at shows in which the American–bred or Open Classes are divided by sex, also shall be divided by sex and each division shall be open only to undefeated dogs of the same sex which have won first prizes in either the Puppy, Novice, Bred–by–Exhibitor, American–bred or Open Classes, excepting only in the event that where either the Puppy, Novice, or Bred–by–Exhibitor Class shall not have been divided by sex, dogs of the same sex winning second or third prizes but not having been defeated by a dog of the same sex may compete in the Winners Class provided for their sex. At shows where the American–bred and Open Classes are not divided by sex there shall be but one Winners Class which shall be open only to undefeated dogs of either sex which have won first prizes in either the Puppy, Novice, Bred–by–Exhibitor American–bred or Open Classes. There shall be no entry fee for competition in the Winners Class.

After the Winners prize has been awarded in one of the sex divisions, where the Winners Class has been divided by sex, any second or third prize winning dog otherwise undefeated in its sex, which however, has been beaten in its class by the dog awarded Winners, shall compete with the other eligible dogs for Reserve Winners. After the Winners prize has been awarded, where the Winners Class is not divided by sex, any otherwise undefeated dog which has been placed second in any previous class to the dog awarded Winners shall compete with the remaining first prize–winners, for reserve Winners. No eligible dog may be withheld from competition.

Winners Classes shall be allowed only at shows where American–bred and Open Classes shall be given.

A member specialty club holding a show for American-bred dogs only may include Winners Classes, provided the necessary regular classes are included in the classification.

A member club holding a show with restricted entries may include Winners Classes provided the regular classes are included in the classification.

Section 10. No Winners Class, or any class resembling it, shall be given at sanctioned matches.

Section 11. Bench show committees may provide such other classes of recognized breeds or recognized varieties of breeds as they may chose, provided they do not conflict with the conditions of the above mentioned classes and are judged before the Best of Breed competition.

Local classes, however, may not be divided by sex in shows at which local group classes are provided.

No class may be given in which more than one breed or recognized variety of breed may be entered, except as provided in these rules and regulations.

Section 12. A club that provides Winners Classes shall also provide competition for Best of Breed or for Best of Variety in those breeds for which varieties are provided in this chapter. The awards in this competition shall be Best of Breed or Best of Variety of Breed.

The following categories of dogs may be entered and shown in this competition: Dogs that are Champions of Record.

Dogs which according to their owners' records have completed the require— ments for a championship but whose championships are unconfirmed. The showing of dogs whose championships are unconfirmed is limited to a period of 90 days from the date of the show where a dog completed the requirements for a championship according to the owners' records.

In addition, the Winners Dog and Winners Bitch (or the dog awarded Winners, if only one Winners prize has been awarded), together with any undefeated dogs that have competed at the show only in additional non—regular classes shall compete for Best of Breed and Best of Variety of Breed.

If the Winners Dog or Winners Bitch is awarded Best of Breed or Best of Variety of Breed, it shall be automatically awarded Best of Winners; otherwise, the Winners Dog and Winners Bitch shall be judged together for Best of Winners following the judging of Best of Breed or Best of Variety of Breed. The dog designated Best of Winners shall be entitled to the number of points based on the number of dogs or bitches competing in the regular classes, whichever is greater. In the event that Winners is awarded in only one sex, there shall be no Best of Winners award.

After Best of Breed or Best of Variety of Breed and Best of Winners have been awarded, the judge shall select Best of Opposite Sex to Best of Breed or Best of Variety of Breed. Eligible for this award are:

Dogs of the opposite sex to Best of Breed or Best of Variety of Breed that have been entered for Best of Breed competition.

The dog awarded Winners of the opposite sex to the Best of Breed or Best of Variety of Breed.

Any undefeated dogs of the opposite sex to Best of Breed or Best of Variety of Breed which have competed at the show only in additional non−regular classes.

Section 13. At specialty shows for breeds in which there are varieties as specified in Chapter 6, Section 1, and which are held apart from all-breed shows, Best of Breed shall be judged following the judging of Best of each variety and best of opposite sex to best of each variety. Best of Opposite Sex to Best of Breed shall also be judged. Dogs eligible for Best of Opposite Sex to Best of Breed competition will be found among the bests of variety or the bests of opposite sex to bests of variety according to the sex of the dog placed Best of Breed.

At an all−breed show (even if a specialty club shall designate classes as its specialty show), the judge of a breed in which there are show varieties shall make no placings beyond Best of Variety and Best of Opposite Sex to Best of Variety.

Section 14. A club or association holding a show may give six group classes not divided by sex, such groups to be arranged in same order and to comprise the same breeds and recognized varieties of breeds as hereinbefore set forth in Chapter 2 and Section 1 of Chapter 6. All dogs designated by their respective breed judges Best of Breed at the show at which these group classes shall be given shall be eligible to compete in the group classes to which they belong according to this grouping, and all dogs designated Best of Variety on those breeds with more than one recognized variety, shall be eligible to compete in the group classes to which they belong according to this grouping. All entries for these group classes shall be made after judging of the regular classes of the American Kennel Club has been finished and no entry fee shall be charged. In the event that the owner of a dog designated Best of Breed or Best of Variety shall not exhibit the dog in the group class to which it is eligible, no other dog of the same breed or variety of breed shall be allowed to compete.

Section 15. A club giving group classes must also give a Best in Show, the winner to be entitled 'Best Dog in Show'. No entry fee shall be charged but the six group winners must compete.

Section 16. A club or association holding a show, if it gives brace classes in the several breeds and recognized varieties of breeds, may also give six brace group classes, not divided by sex; such groups to be arranged in the same order and to comprise the same breeds and recognized varieties of breeds as herein before set forth in Chapter 2 and Section 1 of Chapter 6. All braces of dogs designated by their respective breed judges as Best of Breed or Best of Variety as the case may be at shows at which these brace group classes shall be given, shall be eligible to compete in the brace group classes to which they belong according to this grouping. All entries for these brace group classes shall be made after the judging of the regular classes of the AKC has been finished and no entry fee shall be charged. In the event that the owner of a brace of dogs designated Best of Breed or Best of Variety shall not exhibit the brace of dogs in the group class to which it is eligible, no other brace of dogs of the same breed or variety of breed shall be allowed to compete.

Section 17. If a club or association holding a show shall give these six group classes, it must also give a 'Best Brace in Show' in which the six braces of dogs winning the first prizes in the six group classes must compete, but for which no entry fee shall be charged. The winner shall be entitled 'The Best Brace in Show'.

Section 18. A club or association holding a show, if it gives team classes in several breeds and recognized varieties of breeds, may also give six team group classes not divided by sex, such groups to be arranged in the same order and to comprise the same breeds and recognized varieties of breeds as hereinbefore set forth in Chapter 2 and Section 1 of Chapter 6. All teams of dogs designated by their respective breed judges as Best of Breed or Best of Variety as the case may be at shows at which these team group classes shall be given, shall be eligible to compete in the team group classes to which they belong according to this grouping. All entries for these team group classes shall be made after the judging of the regular classes of the AKC has been finished and no entry fee shall be charged. In the event that the owner of a team of dogs designated Best of Breed or Best of Variety shall not exhibit the team of dogs in the group class to which it is eligible, no other team of dogs of the same breed or variety of breed shall be allowed to compete.

Section 19. If a club or association holding a show shall give these six group classes it must also give a 'Best Team in Show' in which the six teams of dogs winning the first prizes in the six groups must compete, but for which no entry fee shall be charged. The winner shall be entitled 'The Best Team in Show'.

Section 20. A club or association holding a show may give six group classes not divided by sex, open only to local dogs (as designated in its premium list), such groups to be arranged in the same order and to comprise the same breeds and recognized varieties of breeds as hereinbefore set forth in Chapter 2 and Section 1 of Chapter 6. All dogs designated by their respective breed judges 'Best in Local Class of the Breed' or 'Best in Local Class of the Variety of Breed' at the show at which these group classes shall be given shall be eligible to compete in the group classes to which they belong according to this grouping . No entry fee shall be charged. In the event that the owner of the dog designated 'Best in Local Class' shall not exhibit the dog in the group or class in which it is eligible, no other dog of the same breed or variety of breed shall be allowed to compete.

Section 21. A club giving local group classes may also give a 'Best Local Dog in Show'. No entry fee shall be charged but the local group winners must compete.

Section 22. A club or association holding a show may offer Junior Showmanship competition if it so chooses.

   The Classes and procedure shall conform to the AKC regulations governing Junior Showmanship as adopted by the Board of Directors.

Section 23. The Miscellaneous Class shall be for pure-bred dogs of such breeds as may be designated by the Board of Directors of the AKC. No dog shall be eligible for entry in the Miscellaneous Class unless the owner has been granted an Indefinite Listing Privilege, and unless the ILP number is given on the entry form. Application for an Indefinite Listing Privilege shall be made on a form provided by the AKC and when submitted must be accompanied by a fee set by the Board of Directors.

   All Miscellaneous Breeds shall be shown together in a single class except that the class may be divided by sex if so specified in the premium list. There shall be no further competition for dogs entered in this class.

   The ribbons for First, Second, Third and Fourth prizes in this class shall be Rose, Brown, Light Green, and Grey, respectively.

At present the Miscellaneous Class is open to:

Akitas
Australian Cattle Dogs

Australian Kelpies
Bichon Frise

Border Collies
Cavalier King Charles Spaniels
Ibizan Hounds
Miniature Bull Terriers

Soft–coated Wheaten Terriers
Spinoni Italiani
Staffordshire Bull Terriers
Tibetan Terriers

Section 24. A registered dog that is six months of age or over and of a breed for which a classification is offered in the premium list may be entered in a show for Exhibition Only at the regular entry fee provided the dog has been awarded first prize in one of the regular classes at a licensed show or member show held prior to the closing of entries of the show in which the Exhibition Only entry is made, and provided further that the premium list has not specified that entries for Exhibition Only will not be accepted. The name and date of the show at which the dog was awarded the first prize must be stated on the entry form.

A dog entered for Exhibition Only shall not be shown in any class or competition at that show.

German Shepherd Dog Clubs and Associations

The British and American Kennel Clubs each have available comprehensive lists of German Shepherd Dog Clubs and Associations and would be pleased to give details of such clubs in your area. Please remember to enclose a stamped and addressed envelope for their reply.

Selected Bibliography

Few of the following books deal purely and simply with the German Shepherd Dog. Some are concerned with breeding and training, but all contain material which will help readers who may wish to make a serious study of the German Shepherd Dog.

BARBARESI, S. M. *How to Raise and Train a German Shepherd*. New York, 1957

BENNETT and others. *The Complete German Shepherd*. New York, 1970

BROCKWELL, D. *The Alsatian*. n.d.

BURNS, M., and FRASER, M. N. *Genetics of the Dog*. Edinburgh, 1966

CROXTON-SMITH, A. (ed.) *The Kennel*. London, 1910-12

    About Our Dogs. London, 1931

    (ed.) *Hounds and Dogs*. The Lonsdale Library, vol. XIII, London, 1932

DARLING, F. F. *Colour Inheritance in Bull Terriers, The Coloured and Colour Breeding*. Hogarth, Galashiels, 1932

DE BYLANDT, H. *Les Races des Chiens*. Brussels, 1897

DENLINGER, M. G. *The Complete German Shepherd*. Richmond USA, 1952

DODGE, G., and RINE, J. Z. *The German Shepherd Dog in America*. New York, 1956

ELLIOTT, N. *The Complete Alsatian*. London, 1961

    Modern Bloodlines in the Alsatian. London, 1968

FRANKLING, E. *Practical Dog Breeding and Genetics*. London, 1961

GENTRY, J. M. S. (ed.) *The Trainer's Handbook*. London, 1927

GOLDBECKER W., and HART, E. H. *This is the German Shepherd*. Jersey City, 1964

GORON, M. F. *Mémoires de Poum*. Paris, 1913

HAGEDOORN, A. L. *Animal Breeding*. London, 1950

HART, E. H. *Your German Shepherd Puppy*. Jersey City, 1967

HOLMES, J. *Obedience Training for Dogs*. Edinburgh, 1961

HOROWITZ, G. *The Alsatian Wolf-Dog*. Manchester, 1923, and later editions.

HUBBARD, C. L. B. *The Complete Dog Breeder's Manual*. London, 1954

HUTCHINSON'S DOG ENCYCLOPAEDIA. London, 1935

KENWORTHY, J. *Dog Training Guide*. New York, 1969

KNOWLES, G. W. *The Book of Dogs*. London, *c.* 1920

LEIGHTON, R. *The New Book of the Dog*. London, 1907

    The Complete Book of the Dog. London, 1922

LEONARD, L. *Alsatians – (German Shepherd)*. London, 1959

LITTLE, C. C. *The Inheritance of Coat Colour in Dogs*. New York, 1957

LONS, R. *Die Deutschen Schäferhunde*. Magdeburg, 1910

MILLER, M. *German Shepherds as Pets*. London, 1955

MULVANEY, M. *All About Obedience Training*. London, 1973

von OTTO, E. *German Dogs in Word and Picture*. June, 1928

PICKETT, F. N. *The Book of the Alsatian Dog*. London, 1952

PICKUP, M. *The Alsatian Owner's Encyclopaedia*. London, 1964

    German Shepherd Guide. New York, 1969

    All About the German Shepherd Dog. London, 1973

RICHARDSON, E. H. *War, Police and Watch Dogs*. London, 1910
   Watch Dogs, Their Training and Management. London, 1922
RITSON, K. *The Alsatian*. London, 1928
SCHWABACHER, J. *The Popular Alsatian*. London, 1922, and later editions
SCOTT, T. *Obedience and Security Training for Dogs*. London, 1967
SPRAKE, L. *The Art of Dog Training*. London, 1932
von STEPHANITZ, M. *The German Shepherd Dog in Word and Picture*. Jena, 1923
STRICKLAND and MOSES *The German Shepherd Today*. New York, 1974
VESEY-FITZGERALD, B. (ed.) *The Book of the Dog*. London, 1948
WALSH, J. H. ('Stonehenge') *The Dog in Health and Disease*. London, 1859, and later editions
WHITNEY, L. F. *How to Breed Dogs*. New York, 1948
WILLIS, M. B. *The German Shepherd Dog, Its History, Development and Genetics*. Leicester, 1976
WIMHURST, C. G. *The Book of Working Dogs*. n.d.
YOUATT, W. *The Dog*. London, 1845

Glossary of Terms

ABZEICHEN A (*German*) Coat markings.

AFFIX Term applied to a kennel name which is attached to either end of a dog's name in order to identify him with that kennel. The Kennel Club demands that actual *breeders* of the dog or its parents should put the Affix *before* the dog's registered name, while *non-breeders* of the dog should use the Affix as a suffix *after* the dog's registered name.

AHNENTAFEL (*German*) Pedigree.

ALTER (*German*) Age.

ANGULATION The angles formed at the point where the bones meet at the joints. In the hind limb the term refers to the correct angle formed by the true line of the haunch bone, the femur, and the tibia. In the case of the forelegs it refers to the line of the shoulder bone, radius bone, and humerus. A dog which lacks angulation possesses straightness in these joints, and a condition such as this can reasonably be considered unsound.

AOV Any Other Variety. This term indicates that class entries are valid from any other variety than the breed entered for in a previous class.

APPLE HEADED A rounded head such as seen in the top of the skull of the Toy Spaniel. Undesirable in most breeds.

APRON The frill or long hair on the throat and brisket on long-coated breeds.

AUGEN (*German*) Eyes.

AUSBILDUNG (*German*) Training.

AUSDRUCK (*German*) Expression.

AV Any Variety. This term is used to indicate that entries are valid from *any* variety, including those entered for in earlier classes. It applies to 'beauty' shows, stakes, and Field Trials.

B. *or* b. The abbreviation used for bitch (female) in show catalogues.

BAD-DOER A dog who does badly however well fed and cared for, sometimes such a dog has seldom done well from birth.

BAD SHOWER A dog who for reasons of pique, nerves, or boredom will not or cannot display himself properly and well in the show ring.

BAHNDIENSTHUND (BDH) (*German*) Railroad Service Dog.

BALANCE Co-ordination of the muscles providing graceful action coupled with the dog's overall conformation. The lateral dimensions of the specimen should fuse pleasingly with the horizontal and vertical dimensions.

BARRELLED A term referring to the shape of the rib-cage, which should be long, strong, well-rounded, and with plenty of spring, allowing plenty of heart room. This is not the type of ribcage desired in the G.S.D.

BAT EARS Large, pricked ears like a bat's, as seen in the French Bulldog. A fault in many breeds.

BAY The voice or call of a Hound on the trail.

BB Abbreviation for Best of Breed. A dog who has beaten all others in his breed.

BEARD The profuse, bushy whiskers of certain breeds such as the Brussels Griffon.

BEFEHL (*German*) Order or command.

BEHAARUNG (*German*) Coat.

BELEGT (*German*) Mated.

BESITZER (*German*) Owner.

BESITZWECHSEL (*German*) Change of ownership.

BEWERTUNG (*German*) Qualification.

BIS Best in Show.

BITCHY The term for an effeminate or over-refined male dog.

BITE A term referring to the position of the upper and lower incisors when the dog's mouth is closed.

BLAZE A white, usually bulbous, marking running up the centre of the face of some dogs. Some-times the term is used to describe a white collar marking on the coat.

BLINDENFÜHRERHUND (*German*) (abbreviated Bl.H.) Guide dog for the blind.

BLOOM Glossiness or good sheen of coat, suggesting that the dog is in good condition.

BLOCKY Term used to describe the brachycephalic head such as the Boston Terrier's. Sometimes the term is used to describe a short, stocky, cobby body such as the Bulldog's.

BLUE A blue-grey colour as seen on a pigeon and encountered in a number of breeds such as the Whippet and Bedlington Terrier.

BONE A well-boned dog is one with limbs which give the appearance and feel of strength and spring without coarseness.

BOW-HOCKS When the hocks are bent outwards; also termed 'pin-toed'. A fault.

Br. Abbreviation for Breeder, i.e. the owner of the dog's dam at the time of whelping.

BRACE Two dogs or two bitches exhibited together.

BRINDLE A mixture of light and dark hairs, giving a generally dark effect, usually composed of lighter streaks or bars on a grey, tawny, brown, or black background.

BRISKET The part of the body in front of the chest and between the forelegs.

BROKEN COLOUR Where the main coat colour is broken up with white or other coloured hairs.

BROOD BITCH A bitch kept for breeding purposes.

BRUSH A tail which has long bushy hair such as found in the various Spitz breeds.

BRUSTTIEFFE (*German*) Depth of brisket.

BS Abbreviation for Best in Show or Best in Sex; A dog who has beaten all others in the show or all others in his sex.

BURR The irregular formation inside the ear.

BUTTERFLY NOSE When the nostrils are mottled, that is, when they show flesh colour amidst the black or brown pigment.

BUTTON EARS Ears which drop over in front covering the inner cavity, as in the Fox Terrier for example.

CAT FEET Short, round, and tightly-made feet with compact thick pads, the toes well muscled up and arched like a cat's.

CC Challenge Certificate. A Kennel Club award signed by a judge for the best dog of his sex in his breed at a Championship Show.

CD Companion Dog. A dog holding this degree has passed a test for obedience and reliability.

CD (X) Companion Dog (Excellent). A dog holding this degree has passed a severe test for obedience and reliability.

Ch. Abbreviation for Champion. The holder of 3 CCs awarded and signed by three different judges.

CHARACTER A combination of the essential points of appearance and temperament distinctive to the particular breed or variety to which the dog belongs.

CHEEKY Exceptional development of the cheek muscles and cheek tissue.

CHINA EYES Synonymous with Wall Eyes, which are eyes parti-coloured white and blue, uncommon except in such breeds as merle Sheepdogs and some Corgis.

CLODDY A low and thick-set build.

CLOSE-COUPLED Short and nicely-knit in couplings.

COBBY Compact, neat, and muscular in formation, like a cob horse.

CORKY Compact, alert, and lively in body and mind, well-spirited.

COUPLINGS The part of the body between the fore and hind limb joints.

COW HOCKS When the hocks are bent inwards, thus throwing the hind feet outwards. A fault in every breed.

CROUP The area adjacent to the sacrum and immediately before the root of the tail.

CROSS-BREED The progeny of parents of two different pedigree breeds.

CRYPTORCHID A male dog whose testicles are abnormally retained in the abdominal cavity.

CULOTTE The feathery fringe on the back of the forelegs, a term used mainly in breeds such as the Pekingese, Pomeranian, and Schipperke.

CUSHION The fullness of the foreface given by the padding of the upper lips in the Mastiff and Bulldog.

D or d. Abbreviation for the male dog as described in show catalogues etc.

DAM The female parent of puppies. The term is in general use but refers specially to the bitch from the time she whelps the puppies to the time she has finished weaning them.

DECKEN (German) To cover (as by a stud dog).

DECKFARBEX (German) Main colour.

DECKTAG (German) Day for the mating.

DEUTSCHES HUNDESTAMMBUCH (German) Official German Stud Book.

DEW-CLAWS The rudimentary fifth digits and claws found on the insides of the legs below the hocks. If present on the hind legs, they should be removed from the puppies a few days after birth.

DEW-LAP The loose pendulous skin under the throat in some breeds such as the Bloodhound.

DIENSTHUND DH (German) Service dog.

DIENSTSUCHHUND (German) Police dog trained for tracking.

DIMPLES Shallow depressions at each side of the breast bone.

DISH-FACED When a depression in the nasal bone makes the nose higher at the tip than at the stop.

DOME Term applying to the rounded skull in some breeds such as the Spaniel.

DOWN-FACED The opposite of dish-faced, when the nose tip is well below the level of the stop because of a downward inclination of the nose.

DOWN IN PASTERNS Showing an excessive angle of the front feet forward and outward instead of the correct pastern, which whould be slightly angled in line from the forearm to the ground.

DROP EARS Pendant ears which lie close and flat to the side of the dog's cheek or face.

DUDLEY NOSE Wholly flesh-coloured nostrils, usually cherry or coffee-coloured, quite distinct from the Butterfly Nose.

ELBOW, OUT AT When elbows are not close to the body and the points of elbow stick outwards, an unsoundness in most breeds.

ELLENBOGEN (*German*) Elbows.

ELTERN (*German*) Parents.

ENG (*German*) Narrow, tight.

ENKEL (*German*) Grandson.

ENKELIN (*German*) Granddaughter.

ENTIRE A male dog with both testicles descended into the scrotum.

ERSTER (*German*) First.

EXPRESSION A combination of the emplacement, size, colour, and lustre of the eyes which gives the face the aspect desirable to the particular breed or variety.

FAHRTENHUND FH (*German*) Field Trial Trailing dog.

FALL The long hair or fringe overhanging the face of some breeds.

FALSE HEAT A type of heat or season which affects many bitches today. Those affected give every sign of experiencing a normal heat, but the symptoms are liable to disappear suddenly and even if mated a bitch will fail to conceive.

FANG (*German*) Foreface.

FARBE (*German*) Colour.

FASSBEINE (*German*) Barrel or bow-legs.

FASSRIPPE (*German*) Barrel ribs.

FEATHER The long hair or fringe at the back of the legs of some breeds. Sometimes refers to the fringe of hair beneath the tail.

FEHLER (*German*) Faults.

FELTED The term given to a matted coat.

FIDDLE HEAD A long wolf-like head.

FILLED-UP A term given to the face when the cheek muscles are well-developed and depressions under the eyes are filled in with muscle and tissue.

FLAG The long fine hairs beneath the tail. Sometimes refers to the tail itself.

FLANKE (*German*) Loin.

FLARE Another term for blaze.

FLECKED When a coat is slightly ticked or dotted with another colour.

FLEWS The pendulous inner corners of the lips and upper jaw.

FRILL Refers to the hair under the neck and on the chest.

FRONT What can be seen of the dog from the front, especially the chest, brisket and forelegs.

FÜHRER (*German*) Handler.

FURROW The grooves or indentation running from the stop to near occiput in some breeds.

GAIT The dog's walk or movement generally.

GANG (*German*) Gait.

GAY TAIL A tail which is carried horizontally high above level of the back. A fault in the GSD.

GEBRAUCHSHUND (*German*) Working dog.

126

GEDECKT (*German*) Mated.

GESCHLECHT (*German*) Sex.

GESCHUTZTER ZUCHTNAME (*German*) Registered Kennel Name.

GEWINKELT (*German*) Angulated'.

GEWORFEN (*German*) Whelped.

GOOD-DOER A dog which does well at his food and thrives without any special treatment.

GOOSE RUMP When the croup falls away too sharply and abruptly, the tail being set on too low.

GRIZZLE An iron-grey coat colour or a coat colour giving a grizzled grey effect.

GROSSELTERN (*German*) Grandparents.

GROSSMUTTER (*German*) Grandmother (Granddam).

GROSSVATER (*German*) Grandfather (Grandsire).

GUIDE DOG A dog trained to guide blind people.

GUN-SHY A dog who is gun-shy is fearful of a gun or its report.

GUT (*German*) Good.

HAAR (*German*) Coat, Hair.

HACKEN (*German*) Hock.

HALS (*German*) Neck, Throat.

HANDLER A person who handles dogs for exhibition at shows. Although the term can apply to anyone who does this, it usually refers to a professional handler.

HARD-MOUTHED A hard-mouthed dog is one who damages the game he is retrieving; applies to Gundogs.

HARE FOOT A rather long and narrow foot with the digits well separated, as in the Hare.

HARLEQUIN A piebald or patched white and black coat, referring especially to a type of Great Dane.

HAW The inner part of the lower eyelid which, being well developed, hangs down; it often shows red, as in the Bloodhound.

HC Highly Commended. An award in dog shows which indicates an exhibit of high merit but carries (as a rule) no monetary value. Sixth in position.

HEAT A bitch is said to be 'on heat' when she is in season, i.e. during her oestral period.

HEIGHT A dog's height is usually measured vertically from ground to the withers, i.e. to the top of the shoulders.

HINTERLAUFE (*German*) Hind legs.

HITZE (*German*) Heat or Season (of bitch).

HOCKS The joints in the hind legs between the pasterns and stifles, similar to the ankle in humans.

HODEN (*German*) Testicles.

HÖHE (*German*) Height.

HOUND MARKED When the coat colour body patches conform to the conventional pattern of Hounds, i.e. a dark saddle, dark ears and head, and often a patch at or near the set-on of tail. The rest of the coat is white.

HUCKLE BONES The top of the hip joints.

HUND, HÜNDIN, HÜNDCHEN (*German*) Dog, Bitch, Puppy.

IN-BREEDING The mating of closely-related dogs, usually arranged in an attempt to perpetuate certain desirable points already existing in the mating pair.

INTERNATIONAL CHAMPION (abbreviated Int.Ch.) A dog who has been awarded the title of Champion in more than one country; not an officially-recognized term.

INZUCHT (*German*) In-breeding.

KAMPIOEN (*Dutch*) Champion.

KEEL The absolute base of the body, a term usually applied to Dachshunds.

KIND (*German*) Progeny.

KINK-TAIL A tail with a bend or kink in it.

KLEIN (*German*) Small.

KOPF (*German*) Head.

KOPPEL-KLASSE (*German*) Brace Class.

KREIGSHUND (*German*) (abbreviated kr.H.) War Dog; dog trained for Military Service.

KRUPPE (*German*) Croup.

LÄNGE (*German*) Length.

LAÜFE (*German*) Legs.

LAY-BACK The dog's nose when it lies well back into the face, as in the short-faced breeds such as the Bulldog.

LEASH The leather thong by which a dog is held. An old term for three coursing Hounds.

LEATHER The skin of the ear-flap.

LEGGY Term referring to a dog which is high on the leg, making it seem out of balance.

LEISTUNGSIEGER LS (*German*) Field Trial Champion.

LEVEL MOUTH When the jaws are placed so that the teeth meet about evenly, neither undershot nor clearly overshot.

LINE-BREEDING The mating of dogs of near or similar strain, not too closely related.

LIPPY When the dog's lips overhang or are abnormally developed.

LITTER Family of puppies born to the bitch at the same time or whelping.

LOADING Term referring to shoulders which are too heavy.

LOINS That part of the body which protects the lower viscera overlying the lumber vertebrae between last ribs and hindquarters.

LONG-COUPLED The reverse of close-coupled.

LUMBER Too much flesh and weight, giving the dog an ungainly appearance and making it move rather clumsily.

MAIDEN Term that generally refers to an un-mated bitch; it is also used in show circles to indicate an exhibit that has not won a first prize.

MANGELHAFT (*German*) Defective, faulty.

MASK The dark markings on the muzzle, even the muzzle itself.

MASKE (*German*) Mask.

MATCH An elementary form of competition in which one dog is matched against another until all entrants except the winner have ben eliminated.

MATING The act of copulation, when a bitch is served by a dog, i.e. mated.

MATRON A brood bitch, one used for breeding.

MELDEHUND (*German*) Army Messenger Dog.

MERLE Blue-grey colour, usually marbled with black or black flecks, often found in working dogs.

MONORCHID A dog with only one testicle visible and descended into the scrotum.

MUZZLE The projecting part of the head (face) combining mouth and nose.

NAF Name Applied For.

NFC Not for Competition. Abbreviation used on a dog's bench against his entered name in a show catalogue to indicate that he is on display rather than for competition.

NOVICE Usually refers to an inexperienced exhibitor or breeder, but in show world parlance it means a dog or bitch that has not won two first prizes.

OBERARM (*German*) Upper arm.

OCCIPUT That part of the skull at the top and back which is prominent in some breeds, especially the Hound family.

OESTRUM The bitch's menstrual term; sometimes referred to as her 'heat' or 'season'.

OHREN (*German*) Ears.

ON HIS TOES Infers that an exhibit is well-poised, confident, and shows himself well in exhibition.

OUT AT ELBOWS When the points of elbows stick outwards as seen from the front. A fault in most breeds.

OUT AT SHOULDERS When the shoulders protrude outwards in a loose manner giving the effect of a wide front. A fault in most breeds.

OUT-CROSS The mating of dogs which are totally unrelated, although of the same breed.

OVERSHOT When the incisors of the upper jaw project out and beyond the incisors of the lower jaw with a noticeable space between the teeth rows.

P Puppy.

PAD The cushioned or padded sole of the foot.

PARTI-COLOUR A coat of two or more colours in patches or chequered form.

PASTERN The lowest part of the leg below the knee and below the hock, equivalent to the wrist in the human.

PEARK The term applied to the occiput when this is prominent in certain Hounds and Setters.

PEDIGREE A genealogical tree, giving the names of the dog's parents and ancestors, usually to the third or fourth generation.

PFOTE (*German*) Paw.

PIED or PIEBALD Term given to a coat of black and white in roughly equal proportions but placed irregularly over the body.

PIG-JAW A badly overshot jaw, like that of the pig.

PILE The dense undercoat of a long-coated dog.

PLUME The long and feathery soft hair on the tail of a breed such as the Pekingese.

POLITZEIDIENSTHUND Pd.H. (*German*) Dog trained for Police work.

PREFIX An obsolete term for Affix.

PRICKED EARS Ears which stand erect.

QUARTERINGS The junctions of the limbs, especially the hindquarters.

RACY Slight in body build, being rather long cast.

RANG Rather long-bodied, but with some substance yet giving an impression or having loose limbs.

RASSE (*German*) Breed.

RASSEKENNEZEICHEN (*German*) Standard.

RED A general term for the various shades of fawn found in the colours of dogs' coats.

RESERVE The fourth place in awards in a class, as a rule; the term can refer, however, to a runner-up in a class or in a show.

RIBBED-UP A compactly-made dog with well-barrelled ribs.

RING TAIL A curled tail which almost describes a circle.

RIPPEN (*German*) Ribs.

ROACH BACK A back which arches upwards along the spine, starting at the withers and with emphasis over the loins.

ROAN A mixture of white with blue or red in roughly equal proportions and well-placed.

ROSE EARS: Ears which fold over exposing the inner burr.

RUDE (*German*) Male.

SABLE When the outer coat is shaded with black over a light-coloured undercoat, as in the GSD and Collie particularly.

SADDLE A saddle marking of black or brown on the back.

SANITÄTSHUND (*German*) SH. Dog used for Red Cross work.

SCHEU (*German*) Shy.

SCHULTER (*German*) Shoulder.

SCHULTERHÖHE (*German*) Shoulder height.

SCHUTZHUND (*German*) Sch.H. Dog trained for Defence work.

SCHWANZ (*German*) Tail.

SCHWARZGELB (*German*) Black and tan.

SCHWARZGRAU (*German*) Black and grey.

SEASON When a bitch is on heat or menstruating she is said to be in season.

SECOND MOUTH A dog's permanent mouth or teeth, after he has lost his puppy or milk teeth.

SECOND THIGHS The muscular development of the hind legs between the stifles and the hocks.

SEHR GUT (*German*) Very good.

SELF–COLOUR When a dog's coat is of one colour.

SEPTUM The thin line which divides the nostrils.

SERVICE When a bitch is mated by a stud dog she is said to have been served by him; the act of copulation is known therefore as a service.

SET-ON The point where the root of the tail is set on to the hindquarters.

SHELLY Term given to a dog's body which is narrow and shallow.

SHOULDERS Well laid back shoulders, i.e. those with an angle made by the positioning of scapula and humerus. Upright shoulders when the angle is obtuse will produce a mincing gait.

SICKLE HOCKS Hocks which are well bent and let down, as in most breeds built for speed.

SIEGER (m), Siegerin (f) (*German*) Champion.

SIRE The male parent of a dog or bitch.

SNIPY A muzzle which is too long and too weak and pointed.

SOFT MOUTH A dog with a soft mouth is able to retrieve game without damaging it.

SPLAY FEET Feet in which the digits are wide spread.

SPRING A term which refers to elasticity of rib, i.e. when the ribs are well-rounded and elastic.

STANDARD The official description of the breed, drawn up by a panel of experts and approved and published by the Kennel Club. It is used as a guide in judging and breeding.

STAND-OFF The ruff or frill which stands off from the neck of some Spitz breeds.

STERN Another name for tail, used mainly in hunting circles; can refer to a dog's rear end.

STIFLE The joint in the hind leg joining the first and second thighs, roughly equivalent to the knee in humans.

STOP The depression or stop between and in front of the eyes.

STRAIGHT HOCKS Hocks which are virtually straight, and after lacking resilience and bend.

STRAIGHT SHOULDERS Shoulders which are not laid back and lack angulation, causing a dog to move with stiff action.

STRAIGHT STIFLES Stifles which lack bend and render a dog's gait untypical.

STUD DOG A male dog kept mainly for breeding purposes and for which a stud fee is charged to the owner of a visiting bitch.

SUCHHUND SuchH (*German*) Sentry or trailing dog.

SUFFIX When the Affix (or Kennel Name) is joined on the end of a dog's registered name, i.e. 'Rimski *of Rydens*', 'Rydens' being the kennel name used in this instance as a Suffix.

SWAY BACK A back which dips behind the shoulders because of poor muscle structure and development.

TAF Transfer applied for.

TEAM Three or more dogs of any one breed.

THROATY Showing an excess of loose skin about the throat.

TICKING Small marks of another colour appearing on a darker or lighter main coat colour.

TIE The term used to describe the locking union of dog and bitch during copulation.

TIMBER Good bonal and body construction and quality.

TRABEN (*German*) To trot.

TRICOLOUR Three different colours in the coat, referring particularly to black, white, and tan.

TROCKEN (*German*) Dry (referring to bone).

TROUSERS The hair on the hindquarter of a breed such as the Afghan Hound.

TUCKED-UP When the loins are well lifted as in racing and coursing dogs.

TULIP EARS When the ears are carried erect, being slightly open and set at an angle which is slightly forward.

TYPE The quality and appearance essential to a dog if he is to epitomize the ideal model of his breed based on the description given by the particular breed Standard.

UBERWINKELT (*German*) Over-angulated.

UNBEKANNT (*German*) Unknown.

UNDERSHOT When the lower incisors project beyond the upper incisors with a noticeable space between the rows of teeth, as in the Bulldog.

UNSOUND A dog can be said to be unsound if he is unhealthy, unable to fulfil his work, in very bad condition, and fails in movement and true character. A deformed or vicious dog may be deemed permanently unsound, whereas a dog recovering from an accident which has affected his movement may well be temporarily unsound.

UNTERSCHRIFT (*German*) Signature.

URGROSSELTERN (*German*) Great-grandparents.

URGROSSENKEL (*German*) Great-great-grand-son.

URGROSSENKELIN (*German*) Great-great granddaughter.

URGROSSMUTTER (*German*) Great granddam.

URGROSSVATER (*German*) Great grandsire.

VATER (*German*) Father (Sire).

VENT The anus or the area around it.

VEREIN (*German*) Club.

VHC Very Highly Commended; an award in the show ring which gives sixth place but carries no monetary prize.

VORBEISSER (*German*) Undershot.

VORZÜGLICH V (*German*) Excellent.

WALL EYES See China Eyes.

WEEDY Puny and lightly constructed, lacking substance.

WEISS (*German*) White.

WELL-SPRUNG Refers to a dog's ribs when they are well-rounded and have plenty of spring.

WELPE (*German*) Puppy (whelp).

WELTSIEGER (m), WELTSIEGERIN (f) (WS) (*German*) World Champion.

WESEN (*German*) Nature, temperament.

WHEEL BACK An arched or convex back.

WHELPS Newly-born puppies.

WIDERRIST (*German*) Withers.

WITHERS The point where the neck joins the body at the top of the shoulders region.

ZOLLHUND ZH (*German*) Customs Dog.

ZOTTHAARIG (*German*) Shaggy or open coat.

ZUCHTBUCHNUMMER (*German*) Stud Book Number.
ZUCHTPRÜFUNG Z.Pr. (*German*) A Breeding Trial Certificate Test.
ZWEITER (*German*) Second.
ZWERG Z (*German*) Signifies a Miniature Dog in a pedigree.

Index

INDEX

Abbreviations:
BS, Breed Standard; **Ch.,** Champion;
GSD, German Shepherd Dog; **illust.,**
illustrated; **KC,** Kennel Club.

Figures in square brackets [ ] indicate
number of references on page.

Abidec, 72
absorption, 58
action, *see* gait
'Adamant of Viewdowns' (illust.), 59
afterbirth, 62-3, 64-5
Aglactia, 64
Alsace-Lorraine, 14
Alsatian (GSD), 9, 15-16
Alsatian League and Club of Great Britain
    (formerly Alsatian League of Great
    Britain), 15-16, 99
Alsatian, Sheep, Police and Army Dog
    Society (A.S.P.A.D.S.), 16
Alsatian Wolfdog, name used in Britain,
    14, 15
Alsatian Wolfdog, The (G. Horowitz), 10
angulation, 35-6, 101; *see also* gait
Anubis (Egyptian dog of Reincarnation), 9
Any Variety Shows, 93, 98
appearance, general, 34; British BS, 20;
    American BS, 23; German BS, 28-9; in
    shows, 101-4
'Archduke of Rozavel', Ch. (illust.), 43
Arctic regions, GSD in, 9
'Ardra Willow of Timberdown' (illust.),
    102
Armour, Lawrence, 14
Associations and Clubs, 121
A.S.P.A.D.S. (Alsatian, Sheep, Police
    and Army Dog Society), 16
'Astan of Akir' (illust.), 49
'Audifax von Grafath', 10
Augsburg, 12

B.A.A. (British Alsatian Association), 16
back, 34-5; American BS, 25; German BS,
    30
Barker, Mr J.A. and Mrs C.E., 74
Bateman, Lady, 14
Beck, Mrs, 85

bed, size of, 79
benched events, 105
'Beowulf' Z10, 11 [2]
bitch (for breeding), 47-52; age, 53;
    preferred time, 54, 56
body: British BS, 21; American BS, 25;
    German BS, 30
'Bois of Limbrook', W.T. Ch. (illust.), 103
bone, 34
bottomline, 25
Brabazon of Tara, Lord (formerly J.T.C.
    Moore-Brabazon), 14
breech births, 62-3
Breed Shows, 93, 98
Breed Standard, 12, 13, 17-18, 32-40, 48,
    53; S.V., 18, 23; British, 19-22;
    American K.C., 22-7; German, 28-32
breed warden, 12
breeds for American KC Shows, 109-113
breeding, 41-66; methods, 44-7
Breeding and Instruction School of Service
    Dogs, Prussian Government, 12
British Alsatian Association (B.A.A.), 16
British Clubs, 15-16
brush, *see* grooming
Broadbank, Mr B., 94
Bronze Age, 9
Beisswenger, Miss B.L., 23
Bennett, Mr Thomas L., 23
Buchenwald, 16
bulldog, 46
Bush, Mr L., 59

calcium, 64, 72-3
calcium phosphate, 58
Calsimil, 72
Cameron, Mrs J.A., 71
Challenge Certificates, 52, 98, 99, 100,
    104, 105 [3]
Champion's title, 104-5
Championship events, *see* Championship
    Shows; Shows
Championship Shows, 48, 52, 99, 104,
    see also Shows
character: American BS, 23-4; German
    BS, 29
characteristics, British BS, 19; *see also*
    sex characteristics
cheeks: British BS, 20; German BS, 29
chest, 37.

138

stud dog, 47, 52-3, 55, 56-7
Stuttgart, 12
S.V. Club (*der Verein fur deutsche Schaferhunde*), 12; membership of, 13; standard, 18, 23, 28
swiftness, 10

Tail, 35, 50; British BS, 21; American BS, 25; German BS, 30, 32
tapeworm, *see* worming
teats, 63-4, 68
Teck, Duchess of, 15
teeth, 38-9, 49; British BS, 20; American BS, 24; German BS, 30, 32
temperament, 10 [2], 29, 33-4, 53
temperature: of whelping bitch, 61; of room, 61; in cases of Aglactia, 64; in cases of Metritis, 65
Tests for Obedience Classes S(2) (KC), 80-4; Beginners, 80-1; Novice, 81; Class A, 81-2; Class B, 82; Class C, 82-3; Obedience Certificate, 83-4; Explanatory notes, 84-6
'Thekla 1 v.d. Krone', 11
thighs, 36; American BS, 26; German BS, 31
Thompson, Mrs S., 102
Thornton, Mrs Leslie, 15
Thuringia, 10
Tidbold, Mrs M., 96
topline, 35; American BS, 25
training, 15, 73-6; in the home, 74-5; on the lead, 75-6; with children, 76; obedience, 80-92
'Tramella Flame' (illust.), 74
Trimble, Larry, 14
trotting, 26, 28, 29, 51
type, 33

Uglione, Mrs G., 54, 97
'Ullswood Folly', Ch. (illust.), 51
umbilical cord, 62
United States of America, 14
unsoundness, 33, 34, 40

Vaccinations, 16
Verein fur deutsche Schaferhunde, see S.V. Club
veterinary surgeon, 58, 60, 63, 64, 65, 66, 69, 70

Vetzymes, 72
vitamins, 72-3
'Vonjan Nijinsky', Ch. (illust.), 77

Wachsmuth, Herr, of Hanau, 11 [2]
washing, *see* grooming
weaning, 67; diet, 68
weight British BS, 22
whelping, 61-4; first aid supplies for, 61-2; *see also* pre-natal care; post-whelping problems
whelping box, 58-60; (illust.), 60
Whitaker, Mr Percy, 15
Willis, M.B. (*The German Shepherd Dog, its History, Development and Genetics*), 40
Wilson, Mr J., 27
Winfrow, D.D. and R.J., 54
withers: American BS, 25; German BS, 30
wolf, possible origin of GSD, 9-10; mating of GSD with, 9-10; characteristics of, 10
'Wolf of Badenoch', 15
Wolfdog: name used in Britain, 14; name dropped in Britain, 15
working dog, 9
Working Trials: Regulations S(1) Kennel Club, 86-92; Open Working Trials, 87; Championship Working Trials, 87-91; schedule of points, 86-92
worming, 58, 69-70
World War I, dogs used in, 14
World War II, 15
Wurttemburg, 10

Yates, Mr & Mrs, 49
Zuchtbuch (Stud Book), 11, 13